Key Concepts in
Marketing

The SAGE Key Concepts series provides students with accessible and authoritative knowledge of the essential topics in a variety of disciplines. Cross-referenced throughout, the format encourages critical evaluation through understanding. Written by experienced and respected academics, the books are indispensable study aids and guides to comprehension.

JIM BLYTHE

Key Concepts in
Marketing

SAGE

Los Angeles • London • New Delhi • Singapore • Washington DC

First published 2009

SAGE Publications Ltd
1 Oliver's Yard
55 City Road
London EC1Y 1SP

SAGE Publications Inc.
2455 Teller Road
Thousand Oaks, California 91320

SAGE Publications India Pvt Ltd
B 1/I 1 Mohan Cooperative Industrial Area
Mathura Road, Post Bag 7
New Delhi 110 044

SAGE Publications Asia-Pacific Pte Ltd
33 Pekin Street #02-01
Far East Square
Singapore 048763

Library of Congress Control Number: 2008932105

British Library Cataloguing in Publication data

A catalogue record for this book is available from the
British Library

ISBN 978-1-84787-498-6
ISBN 978-1-84787-499-3 (pbk)

Typeset by C&M Digitals (P) Ltd, Chennai, India
Printed in Great Britain by CPI Antony Rowe, Chippenham, Wiltshire
Printed on paper from sustainable resources

FSC
Mixed Sources
Product group from well-managed
forests and other controlled sources

Cert no. SGS-COC-2953
www.fsc.org
© 1996 Forest Stewardship Council

contents

contents

v

key concepts in marketing

alphabetical list of concepts

key concepts in marketing

preface

In the hundred or so years of its existence as an academic subject, marketing has become a complex area of study. At the same time, the practice of marketing has become more sophisticated and a great deal more important in the business world – the old assumption that all a firm needed to do was produce a better product than its competitors has long been discredited.

For students of marketing, the subject is complicated further by the academic debate: as a young discipline, marketing still has to work out its basic concepts, and there is widespread disagreement in the academic community as to what these concepts should be. The aim of this book is to provide a quick reference guide for marketing students, practitioners and academics: it is not a textbook, and does not replace a textbook, but it does provide a quick cross-check so that anyone studying marketing can check the basic definition and academic arguments surrounding the most common concepts in marketing.

The concepts are grouped under four main headings: customers and markets (which outlines the background on which marketing is based), the offer (which is about what the supplier aims to provide in exchange for the customer's cash), approaching customers (which is concerned with the preparation for making the exchange) and promotion (which covers communication with customers). Each section contains the concepts themselves, clearly explained, with cross-references to other related concepts. Of course, all the concepts of marketing are related to a greater or lesser extent – only the most immediate and obvious relationships are linked.

I would like to take this opportunity to thank all the people who have made this book possible. At Sage, Delia Alfonso, Jennifer Pegg and Clare Wells, who have been patient about deadlines, and professional in their support and help. At Plymouth Business School, my friends and colleagues who have made helpful suggestions and supplied ideas. The reviewers, for their approval and helpful suggestions. And finally my wife, Sue, for her support and understanding.

Jim Blythe

preface

Part 1
Customers and Markets

Customer Centrality

> *Customer centrality is the view that the customer's needs, wants and predispositions must be the starting-point for all decision-making within the organisation.*

The idea that the customer should be at the centre of everything we do as marketers is the driving force behind all marketing planning. In any question of marketing, one should always begin with the customer or consumer: in many cases, the customer and the consumer are the same person, but not always. True customer centrality means that the firm should be seeking to create value for customers: this is not done from a sense of altruism, but rather from the viewpoint that, unless we create value for customers, they will not offer value (i.e. money) in return. The concept has been credited to Peter Drucker, who is quoted as saying 'We are all marketers now', and for stating that the sole function of any business is to create a customer. He also said,

> Marketing is so basic that it cannot be considered a separate function. It is the whole business, seen from the viewpoint of its final result, that is, from the customer's point of view.

Customer centrality is a matter of finding needs and filling them, rather than making products and selling them. Putting the customers first is an easy concept to understand: it is fairly obvious that giving poor service or selling shoddy products will cause them to spend their money elsewhere, but the concept is difficult to apply in practice. For example, few firms keep the best spaces in the car park free for customers – these are usually reserved for senior management. Likewise, firms typically express their annual results in financial terms (for the benefit of the shareholders) rather than discussing customer satisfaction ratings, customer retention levels, and so forth.

Narver and Slater (1990) identified three components that determine the degree to which a company is market-orientated: competitor orientation, customer orientation and inter-functional co-ordination. For these authors, customer orientation is the degree to which the organisation understands its customers. The better the understanding, the better the firm is able to create value for the customers.

Understanding customers is, however, only the beginning. Customers can be seen to have generic needs: these are as follows:

- **Current product needs**. All customers for a given product have needs based on the product features and benefits. They may also have similar needs in terms of the quantity of product they buy, and any problems they might face in using the product (for example, complex equipment such as GPS units may need specialised instruction manuals).
- **Future needs**. Predicting future needs of existing customers is a key element in customer orientation. Typically, this is a function of marketing research, but part of the customer centrality concept is that we should not tire out our customers by constantly asking them questions – some people resent being asked about their future needs, even though the firm might only be trying to be helpful.
- **Desired pricing levels**. Customers naturally want to buy products at the lowest possible prices, but pricing is far from straightforward for marketers. Customers will only pay what they think is reasonable for a product, and obviously firms can only supply products at a profit (at least in the long term). Customers will only pay what they perceive as a 'fair' price (based on what they believe to be the benefits of owning the product), but equally, price is a signal of quality: people naturally assume that a higher-priced product represents better quality. Thus cutting prices might be counter-productive, since it signals that the product is of lower quality.
- **Information needs**. Customers need to know about a product, and about the implications of owning it: this includes the drawbacks as well as the advantages. In most cases, companies are unlikely to flag up the drawbacks (except regarding unsafe use of the product) but customers will still seek out this information, perhaps from other purchasers and users of the product. Information therefore needs to be presented in an appropriate place and format, and should be accurate.
- **Product availability**. Products need to be available in the right place at the right time. This means that the firm needs to recruit the appropriate intermediaries (wholesalers, retailers, agents and so forth) to ensure that the product can be found in the place the customer expects to find it.

The above needs are generic to all customers, whether they are commercial customers, consumers, people buying on behalf of family or friends, or even organisational buyers.

The concept of customer centrality is not easy to apply within firms, because managers have to balance the needs of other groups of stakeholders. Company directors have a legal responsibility to put shareholders' interests ahead of any other consideration, personnel managers have a responsibility to meet the needs of employees, and so forth. The main difficulty (and one which eludes many marketers) is the reasoning behind customer centrality. Some marketers tend to believe that meeting customer needs effectively is an end in itself, whereas others see it as instrumental in persuading customers to part with their money. This is by no means an abstract difference of view – marketers taking the former view will tend to think of all customers as being worthy of attention, whether they are profitable customers or not, whereas those adhering to the second viewpoint will take a much more cynical view, perhaps appearing to seek to exploit customers. For example, Sir Alan Sugar (the hard-nosed London entrepreneur who built the Amstrad consumer electronics business up from nothing within a few years) is famous for saying 'Pan Am takes good care of you. Marks & Spencer loves you. Securicor cares. At Amstrad, we want your money' (*Financial Times* 1987).

Although Sugar's statement was perhaps somewhat tongue-in-cheek, it does sum up the underlying attitude of many company directors. In this view of the world, the purpose of meeting customer needs is to ensure that customers are still prepared to hand over their money in exchange for value received – a concept that has not eluded Sugar, whose products always represent good value for money.

In 2000 Peter Doyle published a seminal book entitled *Value-Based Marketing* in which he critiqued the idea of customer centrality. The aim of the book was to redefine the role of marketing and clarify how its success (or otherwise) should be measured. His argument was that marketing has not been integrated with the modern concept of value creation: it is still caught up in the profit-making paradigm, which is not actually what companies do: in the main, companies are focused on maximising shareholder value.

Doyle gave numerous examples of companies that had succeeded not through exceptional consumer value, but through creating and providing exceptional value to other stakeholders. He pointed out that only 12 chief executives of the UK's top 100 companies had any marketing experience, and 43% of UK companies had no marketing representation on their board of directors. Doyle attributes this to a failure of marketers to take on board the concept of shareholder value, which is (in general) the main preoccupation of boards of directors. In fact, Doyle regards this as the primary obligation of directors. This leads on to the idea that marketing is, in fact, a means to an end: providing customer value is only a stage in the process of increasing shareholder value.

In the final analysis, customer centrality is an easy (even obvious) concept, but the practical difficulties of implementing it are immense. Marketers will, in the meantime, continue to advocate the idea that customer need should be foremost in corporate thinking, and company directors will continue to regard customers as only one stakeholder group. Probably the directors are right – but even if this is the case, customers are the only stakeholder group that provides the income the company needs to fund all the other stakeholders. That being the case, other stakeholders need to consider what they are offering which will facilitate the exchanges with customers on which the company relies.

See also: relationship marketing, consumerism, the whole of Part 3

REFERENCES

Doyle, P. (2000) *Value-Based Marketing*. Chichester: John Wiley.
Financial Times (1987) Also reported in *The Observer* (3 May 1987) 'Sayings of the week'.
Narver, J.C. and Slater, S.F. (1990) 'The effects of a market orientation on business profitability', *Journal of Marketing*, 54 (Oct): 20–55.

customers and markets

6

Management of Exchange

Management of exchange is the theory that marketing is concerned with influencing and controlling the transfer of value between buyers and sellers.

The view of marketing as the management of exchange is usually associated with Philip Kotler, who defines marketing as follows:

> Marketing is a social and managerial process by which individuals and groups obtain what they need and want through creating and exchanging products and value with others. (Kotler et al., 2003)

In fact, the exchange view of marketing was first proposed by Wroe Alderson (1957), and is based on the assumption that both parties want what the other one has, and are both prepared to exchange.

Exchange as a means of obtaining what one wants goes back to prehistory. Even before formalised trading was invented we can assume that early people exchanged surpluses of one thing for other things they needed. In the Lake District region of the UK a prehistoric factory for making hand axes was discovered in the 1960s: axes made from Lakeland stone have been found as far away as the South of France, so fairly obviously a flourishing trade of some sort existed during the Stone Age.

Economists have developed theories of exchange which seek to explain the process and motivations of those involved. The key concept is that of the indifference curve, which illustrates the degree to which someone is prepared to accept a surplus of one item in exchange for another.

An indifference curve assumes that an individual has a trade-off between different items in his or her portfolio of wealth. For example, most people have a store of food in their houses, and a store of money in the bank. Up to a point, it does not matter much if one spends some of the money (reducing the store of cash) in order to increases the store of food, but as the imbalance grows the level of food that needs to be bought to compensate for the reduction in savings will have to increase. In other words, if the freezer is already full, the consumer would have to see a really irresistible bargain in frozen turkeys in order to make the purchase. The same is true in the other direction – if food stocks go too low, the individual will certainly spend a portion of his or her savings to restock the larder, and the bank would have to offer an extremely high interest rate to prevent this happening. An indifference curve which illustrates this is shown in Figure 1.1. Note that the curve ends before it reaches the limit – this is because the individual will have a cut-off point, not wishing to have no money at all but plenty of food, or no stocks of food but plenty of money.

If we consider a simple case of two individuals, each of whom has a supply of food and a supply of money, we can map the total supply of

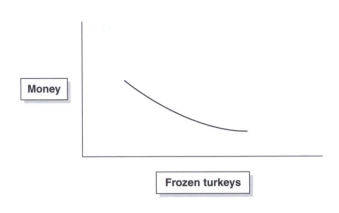

Figure 1.1 *Indifference curve*

food and money as shown in Figure 1.2. Here, Person A and Person B are each indifferent as to how much food or money they have, provided the totals fall somewhere along the indifference curve. However, it is possible to consider Point C, which is a point at which the total amount of food and money could be divided between the two people, but which lies above each of their indifference curves. This means that both are actually better off in terms of both food and money. Point C is on the contract line, which is a line along which either party would be better off. Note that the nearer Point C is to an individual's indifference curve, the better off the other individual will be, so the actual point at which

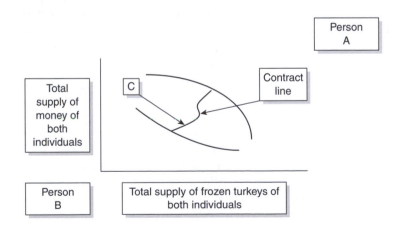

Figure 1.2 *Edgeworth Box*

the exchange is made will depend on the negotiating skills or power relationships of the parties. In the diagram, Person B is obviously not as skilled a bargainer as Person A. This model was first proposed by Edgeworth (1881) and refined by Pareto in 1906, so it considerably pre-dates either Wroe Alderson or Philip Kotler.

At first, it appears counter-intuitive that an exchange results in both parties being better off in terms of both money and turkeys. This apparent anomaly comes about because each individual has a different view of the relative values of food and money. This is clearly the case if the individuals are, respectively, a grocer and a consumer. The grocer would rather have the money than have the food, since he or she has more than enough food for personal use, whereas the consumer would clearly prefer to have the food rather than the money. This concept is important because it negates the idea that market value is fixed. All values are subjective, and depend on the perceptions and situation of the individual.

Broadly then, trade is always good and exchanges always result in both parties being better off (except in the case of deliberate fraud, of course). This is why governments worldwide try to reduce trade barriers: the more we trade with other countries, the better off we become.

Returning to Kotler's definition of marketing, there is a problem in that it tries to include all human exchange processes, and does not differentiate between the buyer and the seller. This makes the definition very broad, which means that it is difficult to identify what is marketing and what is not (presumably this is what a definition sets out to do). For example, Kotler is apparently arguing that a parent who agrees to take a child to the cinema in exchange for tidying his room is engaging in marketing, and even that the child is also engaging in marketing. This would seem somewhat peculiar to most people.

A further criticism of the marketing-as-exchange-management model is that it does not allow for non-profit marketing, unless one is prepared to stretch a few points intellectually. If a government anti-drinking campaign uses a series of TV advertisements to discourage people from over-indulging, this is clearly marketing (within the non-profit marketing paradigm). However, it is difficult to see where the exchange part of the equation comes in. Is someone who heeds the advertising and reduces his or her drinking actually giving the government something in exchange for the advertising? And what (if anything) is the exchange being offered?

Undoubtedly marketing involves the management of exchange as part of what it does. Managing exchange is not the whole of marketing, though, nor do all exchanges fit under the marketing umbrella.

See also: quality, the whole of Part 2

REFERENCES

Alderson, W.C. (1957) *Marketing Behaviour and Executive Action: A Functionalist Approach to Marketing*. Homewood, IL: Irwin.

Edgeworth, F.Y. (1881) *Mathematical Psychics*. Kegan Paul.

Kotler, P., Armstrong, J., Saunders, J. and Wong, V. (2003) *Principles of Marketing*. Harlow: FT Prentice Hall.

Pareto, V. *Manual of Political Economy*. London: Macmillan.

Evolution of Marketing

The evolution of the marketing model seeks to explain how marketing theory and practice have progressed over the past 150 years: it also offers alternative business paradigms which are in evidence today.

Marketing is popularly supposed to have gone through a series of evolutionary stages before arriving at the marketing concept (the view that everything the company does should be driven by market forces, and ultimately by customer needs). Keith (1960) outlined one model of how marketing practice developed, based on the Pillsbury Dough Company, a large American flour milling company. Keith said that the company had gone through three distinct paradigms in the course of developing a marketing concept. These were as follows:

1 **The production era.** At this time the capacity of the mills rather than customer need was what drove the market. The reason for this was that the market was growing rapidly, so that demand outstripped supply.

2   **The sales era**. During this period, the company regarded an effective, fast-talking sales force as the way to control the market.
3   **The marketing era**. At this time the company was driven by customer need.

Although this model was referring to a very specific company at a very specific time, it has become the main model quoted in textbooks and on marketing courses. The basic model has itself evolved over time, as follows:

(1) Production orientation is the view that the route to corporate success lies in production efficiency, getting production costs as low as possible (usually by manufacturing in very large volume) in order to reduce costs and prices. This orientation had its beginnings at the start of the Industrial Revolution. Up until the nineteenth century, almost everything was hand-made and made to measure. Clothing was produced by tailors to almost exact measurements or was made at home, houses and vehicles were produced to customer specification, and relatively few items were standardised. Producing in this way is relatively expensive, consequently prices were high for most goods and people owned correspondingly fewer things. When machines were introduced to speed up the manufacturing process, costs dropped to perhaps one-tenth of the cost of customised products, so that prices could also be cut provided enough goods could be sold. The longer the production run, the lower the costs and consequently the greater the profit: customers were prepared to accept items that were not exactly meeting their needs, since prices were a fraction of what they would have had to pay for the perfect, tailor-made article. For manufacturers, the key to success was therefore ever more efficient (and low-cost) production, but at the cost of meeting individual customers' needs.

Production orientation still survives in some markets, notably those where most people do not already own the core benefits of the products concerned. Until recently production orientation was the prevailing manufacturing paradigm in Communist countries, but this is now being replaced by a more market-oriented approach.

(2) Product orientation is the view that an ideal product can be produced that will have all the features any potential customer might want. This orientation is thought to be a result of oversupply of basic goods. Once everyone already owned the core benefits of the products concerned, manufacturers needed to provide something different in order to find new customers. Products with more features, made to a higher standard, began to be

introduced. By the late nineteenth century extravagant claims were being made for products on the basis of their quality and features. Manufacturers sought to resolve the problem of diverse customer need by adding in every possible feature. The drawback of this approach is that the price of the product increases dramatically, and customers are not always prepared to pay for features they will never use. Modern examples of product orientation include the Kirby vacuum cleaner, which has a multitude of features and can clean virtually anything, and Microsoft Windows software. The end price of the Kirby cleaner is perhaps ten times that of a basic vacuum cleaner, a price that most people are unable or unwilling to pay. In the case of Windows software, the marginal cost of adding extra features to the CD set is tiny compared with the cost of producing separate CDs for each customer group, so it is vastly more efficient to send out everything to everybody and allow each customer to install and use the features they need.

The difficulty with both production orientation and product orientation is that they do not allow for the different needs and circumstances of consumers. Customers differ from each other in terms of their needs – there is no such thing as 'the customer'.

(3) Sales orientation is based on the idea that manufacturing companies can produce far more goods than the market can accept. Sales-oriented companies assume that people do not want to buy goods, and will not do so unless they are persuaded to do so: such companies concentrate on the needs of the seller rather than the needs of the buyer. Sales orientation relies on several assumptions: first, that customers do not really want to spend their money: second, that they must be persuaded by the use of hard-hitting sales techniques: third, that they will not mind being persuaded and will be happy for the salesperson to call again and persuade them some more: and fourth, that success comes through using aggressive promotional techniques.

Sales orientation is still fairly common, especially in firms selling unsought goods such as home improvements and insurance, and often results in short-term gains. In the longer term, customers will judge the company on the quality of its products and after-sales service, and (ultimately) on value for money. Sales orientation should not be confused with the practice of personal selling: successful salespeople do not operate on the basis of persuasion, but rather on the basis of identifying and meeting individual customers' needs.

(4) Marketing orientation means being driven by customer needs: this is sometimes also called customer orientation. Companies that are

truly marketing oriented will always start with the customer's needs, whatever the business problem. Customers can be grouped according to their different needs, and a slightly different product offered to each group. This type of differentiation allows the company to provide for the needs of a larger group in total, because each target segment of the market is able to satisfy its needs through purchase of one or other of the company's products. The underlying assumption of marketing orientation is that customers want to satisfy their needs, and will be willing to buy products that do so. Customer need includes a need for information about the products, advice about product usage, availability of products and so forth. Customer need therefore goes beyond the basic core benefits of the product itself. For example, research has shown that most American consumers no longer know how to choose fresh meat and vegetables, so they seek the reassurance of a well-known brand, or the local supermarket's guarantee of quality. This has encouraged farmers and others in the food industry to provide the type of quality assurance modern consumers need (Stanton and Herbst, 2005).

Marketing orientation also implies that customer needs are the driving force throughout the organisation. Decisions within the organisation, in every department from manufacture through to delivery, need to be taken in consideration of customer needs at every stage. Quality control in the factory, accurate information given by telephonists and receptionists, and courteous deliveries by drivers all play a part in delivering customer value. Narver and Slater (1990) identified three components that determine the degree to which a company is marketing-orientated: competitor orientation, customer orientation and inter-functional co-ordination.

(5) Societal marketing includes the concept that companies have a responsibility for the needs of society as a whole, so should include environmental impact and the impact of their products on non-users (Kotler et al., 2003). Societal marketers believe that sustainability is a key issue since it is of no help to the long-term survival of the firm if natural resources are used too quickly. Long-term results of use of the product are also considered, in terms of their impact on the environment. For example, a car manufacturer might aim to make cars quieter in operation rather than simply improving the soundproofing for its occupants and ignoring the needs of people who live near major roads.

There is some doubt among academics as to whether the marketing concept actually evolved in this linear manner at all. In 1988 Fullerton put forward two main arguments against the idea that the nineteenth century was characterised by the production era. First, the model ignores historical facts about business conditions at the time, which were in fact unstable and often characterised by sharp falls in demand: there were several major depressions between 1870 and 1920. Second, the production-era idea assumes that demand was stimulated by dramatically cheaper production, but in fact the nineteenth century was characterised by aggressive marketing activities. Hard-selling shop assistants and advertising that made outrageous claims about the products were common.

The evidence for the existence of a sales era is also dubious. Marketing, as opposed to selling, activities were well established long before the sales era was supposed to have occurred, and many companies were already considering customers' needs during this era. The hard-sell techniques that supposedly characterised the sales era are certainly still in use nowadays, and the problem-solving approach used by modern salespeople was in evidence even in the so-called sales era.

Of course, the prevailing climate of business might be that one or other paradigm comes to the fore, even though there are exceptions: inevitably, there would always be a degree of overlap in the course of a paradigm shift. On the other hand, Gilbert and Bailey (1990) re-thought the history of marketing and developed an alternative model. This is as follows:

1 **The era of antecedents (1500–1750).** During this period commerce developed from an activity that was regarded as little better than fraud to become a respectable profession. This period also saw the growth of capitalism, whereby people with money could invest in companies without being involved in managing the business. The separation of management from investment was an important step in professionalizing managers.

2 **The era of origins (1750–1850).** During this period the basic concepts of marketing began to develop. Segmentation and advertising began to grow in importance, competition became intense, and markets became considerably less stable.

3 **The era of institutional development (1850–1930).** During this period specialist institutions such as large retailers and wholesalers, commercial services such as accountants and lawyers, and specialist distribution systems such as rail and road freight transporters grew up to serve the needs of industry.

4 **The era of refinement and formalisation (1930–present).** During this period academics began to study marketing in a formal way, and general theories about markets began to evolve. Consequently, marketing also became a distinct profession, with trained marketers who had degrees and diplomas in the subject.

Clearly there are many other possibilities for explaining the development of the marketing concept: history is not an exact science. There is little doubt that the various paradigms have existed and indeed do still exist: what is in doubt is whether they represent a linear evolution.

See also: *relationship marketing, postmodern marketing*

REFERENCES

Fullerton, R.A. (1988) 'How modern is modern marketing? Marketing's evolution and the myth of the production era', *Journal of Marketing,* 52 (Jan): 108–25.

Gilbert, D.C. and Bailey, N. (1990) 'The development of marketing – a compendium of historical approaches', *Quarterly Review of Marketing,* 15 (2): 6–13.

Keith, Robert J. (1960) 'The marketing revolution', *Journal of Marketing,* 24 (Jan): 35–8.

Kotler, P., Armstrong, G., Saunders, J. and Wong, V. (2003) Principles of marketing. Harlow: FT Prentice Hall.

Narver, J.C. and Slater, S.F. (1990) 'The effects of a market orientation on business profitability', *Journal of Marketing,* 54 (Oct): 20–55.

Stanton, John L. and Herbst, Kenneth C. (2005) 'Commodities must begin to act like branded companies: some perspectives from the United States', *Journal of Marketing Management,* 21 (1/2): 7–18.

Relationship Marketing

> *Relationship marketing is the paradigm under which customers are valued for their lifetime potential, rather than for a single transaction or even a series of transactions.*

For the past 20 years relationship marketing has been building towards being the accepted paradigm of marketing. Essentially, relationship marketing states that it is better and cheaper to keep an existing customer than to expend effort on recruiting new ones. Theodore Levitt first outlined the principles of relationship marketing, suggesting that marketers should focus on the lifetime value of the customer rather than on the single transaction (Levitt, 1983).

Customer retention has become increasingly recognised as the key to long-term survival. In the past, most companies have operated on a 'leaky bucket' basis, seeking to refill the bucket with new customers while ignoring the ones leaking away through the bottom of the bucket (Ehrenberg, 1988) (see *leaky bucket theory*, p. 20). According to research by Gupta et al. (2004), a 1% improvement in customer retention will lead to a 5% improvement in the firm's value. A 1% improvement in marginal cost or in customer acquisition cost only make a 1% increase in firm value respectively. In other words, according to Gupta et al., customer retention is five times as effective as cutting costs.

Reichheld (1996) found that, in US corporations, 50% of customers are lost over five years, 50% of employees are lost in four years and 50% of investors are lost in less than a year. Firms therefore need to recognise and reward loyal customers and ensure (as far as possible) that they remain as customers of the company's products.

Traditional marketing is concerned with the exchanges between organisations and their customers, and therefore tends to focus on producing products that satisfy consumers' immediate needs. This in turn leads to a focus on the single transaction, and on acquiring new customers, either from the same market segment or from new ones. The inherent assumption is that customers who have bought once will naturally buy again, unless they are dissatisfied for some reason. Since most marketing transactions occur anonymously (even the retailers do not usually know which customers have bought which products) the customer is reduced from being an individual with individual needs and wants to being a member of a market segment.

Relationship marketing focuses on the lifetime value of the customer. For example, a motorist might own 30 or more cars over a lifetime of driving, representing an expenditure of hundreds of thousands of pounds, yet few manufacturers or car dealers try to keep in touch with their customers in any organised way. Their interest is only in each individual transaction rather than in creating loyalty. Relationship marketing seeks to value the loyal customer ahead of the one-off deal, and seeks to

Transaction marketing	Relationship marketing
Focus on the single sale	Focus on customer retention
Orientation on product features	Orientation on product benefits
Short time-scales	Long time-scales
Little emphasis on customer service	High emphasis on customer service
Limited customer commitment	High customer commitment
Moderate customer contact	High customer contact
Quality is the concern of the production department	Quality is the concern of all

Figure 1.3 *Transaction* vs. *relationship marketing*

build a loyal customer base over a long period. Figure 1.3 shows the comparison between transaction and relationship marketing.

Transactional approaches tend to lead to the following bad practices:

- **A reactive approach to customer complaints**. Rather than confirming with customers that they are happy with the firm's products and services, and thus encouraging people to voice their complaints, transaction-orientated firms tend to wait until customers go out of their way to inform the company that there is a problem.
- **Failure to recognise the needs of long-term customers**. Customers increasingly expect their custom to be valued, and expect loyalty to be rewarded. Transaction-orientated firms do not do this.
- **Greater expenditure on promotion than is necessary**. Spending to attract new customers is generally higher than promoting to known, existing customers simply because a 'scattergun', mass approach is needed.
- **Inner conflicts between departments**. In transaction-orientated firms the production people tend to expect marketers to go out and sell the products that they make, whereas marketers tend to expect production people to make products that will sell. If the organisation is orientated around creating long-term relationships, production people are likely to be directly involved with the customers, at one or another level.

A related concept is customer intimacy. This means getting as close to the customer as possible in order to understand his or her needs as clearly as possible. Being able to think like the customer is a key skill in establishing and maintaining the relationship, and there is a strong positive relationship between marketing orientation and customer intimacy (Tuominen et al., 2004).

The evidence is that the relationship marketing process works much better in business-to-business (B2B) markets than in business-to-consumer markets. This is almost certainly because the needs of a business change much more slowly than the needs of an individual. Businesses make the same basic things year after year, they use the same raw materials, operate the same systems and do not (in general terms) grow old and die. There are many businesses that are over a hundred years old, still producing much the same products, and still bidding fair to become two hundred years old or more. People live about seventy to eighty years, and for much of this time they are not of much interest economically, either because they are too young or because they are too old or because they do not have much money. Relationship marketing, therefore, is a simple concept that is difficult to apply in practice.

Another reason for the greater success of relationship marketing in B2B is that professional buyers are operating in a relatively high-risk situation because they are spending other people's money, and might be called to account for any mistakes. This naturally leads them to continue to buy from a recognised and trusted supplier, rather than risk switching to a new one.

From the supplier's viewpoint, there are clear advantages to being on the 'approved supplier' list of a company, and it is therefore worthwhile to go to some trouble to lock-in the customer. On the other hand, in business-to-consumer markets, suppliers need to be much more circumspect because customers can switch suppliers so much more easily.

Establishing good relationships has been compared to courtship and marriage (Levitt, 1983). Marriage is generally regarded as a relationship of equals, though, and most business relationships are unlikely to be very equal. One or other partner almost always has the upper hand, either because of size and buying power or because there are many competing suppliers. Adaptation tends to be one-sided, therefore, and the evidence is that suppliers are much more likely to adapt their business approach than are buyers (Brennan et al., 2003). The reasons are as follows:

- **Relative power**. Buyers are usually in a position of power, especially in B2B markets, since they can always spend their money elsewhere.
- **Buyer support**. Buying companies will often help suppliers to make the necessary changes in their practices: for example, a motor manufacturer might supply design services to a component manufacturer in order to ensure that products are made to an exact specification.
- **Managerial preference for a more (or less) relational exchange**. Suppliers typically want to get close to their customers to ensure continuity of orders, but the pressure on buyers to get close to suppliers is considerably less.

Most firms have many suppliers and even more customers, so it is impossible to develop the kind of close relationship one has with one's spouse. In a marriage, one adapts what one does to fit the needs of the other person (the perfect marketing approach, in fact) but in consumer markets, where there are thousands or even millions of consumers, this is not possible. Marketers are forced to offer a standard response, or even a range of standard responses, which necessarily are less than perfect. Caroline Tynan has suggested that the relationship does not in fact bear much similarity to marriage: in most cases it appears to have more in common with seduction and polygamy (Tynan, 1997). From a consumer's viewpoint, many companies are acting more like stalkers than like lovers. Some firms, especially credit card companies and similar financial services companies, are apt to jump out from behind the bushes when you least expect them, all in the name of customer retention.

Another aspect of relationship marketing is the cost of 'divorce'. The cost of switching suppliers is generally not as high as the cost of finding new customers, so again the relationship is unlikely to be one of equals: the situation favours the buyers, who have (usually) much lower switching costs than do the suppliers.

Finally, relationship marketing has been criticised for its emphasis on lifetime value of customers, this can lead, in some cases, to ignoring or devaluing customers who have a relatively short remaining life for the company – older people, for example, can be discounted because they have a relatively short period of life remaining in which to make purchases. This thinking can mean that a large and wealthy group can be by-passed entirely.

All of these criticisms have been levelled at relationship marketing theory. Establishing long-term relationships is known to be a good idea for most companies, but in practice it seems to be more elusive than most firms expect.

See also: leaky bucket theory, evolution of marketing

REFERENCES

Brennan, Ross D., Turnbull, Peter W. and Wilson, David T. (2003) 'Dyadic adaptation in business-to-business markets', *European Journal of Marketing*, 37 (11): 1636–45.

Ehrenberg, A.S.C. (1988) *Repeat Buying: Facts, Theory and Applications*. London: Charles Griffin.

Gupta, Sunil, Lehmann, Donald R. and Stuart, Jennifer Ames (2004) 'Valuing customers', *Journal of Marketing Research*, 41 (1): 7–18.

Levitt, T. (1983) 'After the sale is over', *Harvard Business Review*, Sept–Oct, 87–93.

Reichheld, F. (1996) *The Loyalty Effect*. Boston, MA: Harvard Business School Press.

Tuominen, Matti, Rajalo, Arto and Møller, Kristian (2004) 'Market-driving versus market-driven: divergent roles of market orientation in business relationships', *Industrial Marketing Management*, 33 (3): 207–17.

Tynan, C. (1997) 'A review of the marriage analogy in relationship marketing', *Journal of Marketing Management*, 13 (7): 695–703.

The Leaky Bucket Theory

> **The leaky bucket theory is the model that seeks to describe the process of customer gain and loss, otherwise known as customer churn.**

Customer retention is one of the key concepts in relationship marketing. Most companies concentrate on recruiting new customers to replace customers who move on, rather than seeking to retain customers. Andrew Ehrenberg coined the phrase 'leaky bucket' to describe this syndrome: in effect, firms are putting customers into a leaky bucket, and instead of preventing them from leaking away through the bottom of

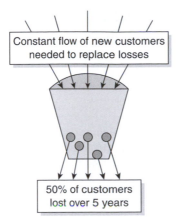

Figure 1.4 *The leaky bucket*

the bucket, the firm keeps topping up the bucket with new customers (Ehrenberg, 1988).

A study performed by the Cumberland Bank (Murphy, 2001) in the United States showed that the top 5% of the customer base accounted for 40% of total deposits, that a 5% increase in retention of top customers added 4% to the bank's profitability, and the minimum balance of the top 20% of customers is $20,000.

The problem with leaky bucket theory is that the analogy is not exact. There will always be a certain amount of customer churn simply because customers' needs change, or they die (or go bankrupt in the case of business customers), or they move away. Also, the cost of plugging the leaks may be higher in some cases than the cost of recruiting new customers: this depends on the industry, the customer base, the costs of recruiting new customers, and so forth. Finally, it is certainly the case that some customers are not worth retaining, since they cost the company more to service than they contribute in terms of revenue.

See also: *relationship marketing*

21

REFERENCES

Ehrenberg, A.S.C. (1988) *Repeat Buying: Facts, Theory and Application.* London: Charles Griffin.

Murphy, J.A. (2001) *The Lifebelt: The Definitive Guide to Managing Customer Retention.* Chichester: Wiley.

Postmodern Marketing

> **Postmodern marketing is the application of postmodern philosophy to aspects of marketing activities and concepts.**

Modernism is the view that the human race is progressing, growing and moving towards a better future from a somewhat less convenient past. This has been the prevailing view in marketing: for example, the Boston Consulting Group Matrix assumes that markets will continue to grow, albeit at different rates. Modernism is typified by the word 'progress', and indeed it is a philosophy that embraces individualism, freedom, advancement and a rejection of the hidebound past represented by religion, myth and tradition.

Postmodernism is a philosophical standpoint that says the human race is not progressing at all, but merely living in the present. Different ways of life, different styles, different attitudes are all mixed in together in a pluralist world: there is no dominant style. At the same time, the future and the past become confused, and we may well move towards the past (for example, we have retro designs such as the new Volkswagen Beetle) or try to live in the future (becoming a science fiction fan, perhaps). There is a cultural propensity to juxtapose almost anything with almost anything else, whether it fits or not (Salsa music, for example, is a fusion of jazz and Latin music). Postmodernists also believe that chaos and disequilibria are normal (rather than order and equilibrium). This view accords well with the idea of hypercompetition.

Almost all postmodern ideas seem to fit extremely well with the current state of play in marketing (Brown, 1997). For example, consumption and production are often reversed – people define themselves by what they consume, not by what they produce, and the emphasis in the developed world (the post-industrial world) is mainly on consumption. Few of us produce anything in any physical sense. Then again, there is a lack of commitment (very postmodern) in which people are reluctant to commit to anything at all, whether it's an idea or a brand or a project.

The features of postmodernism, and their relationship to marketing, are as follows. This list is based on Firat and Shultz (1997):

- **Openness/tolerance**. This is the acceptance of different styles and ways of living without prejudice or evaluations of superiority or inferiority. In marketing, this openness to new ideas has made it much easier to find 'new, improved' products simply by transferring ideas in from other cultures. This is especially true in the food industry.
- **Hyperreality**. This is the constitution of social reality through hype. Hyperreality refers to overstatement: for example, the slogan 'Rowntrees Fruit Pastilles Take You Beyond Fruit' is hyperreal. Marketers use hyperreal statements frequently in advertising pitches, so much so that UK law refers to 'advertising puff' as being acceptable in law (although of course outright lies are not acceptable).
- **Perpetual present**. In the postmodern world, we experience everything in the present, whether it is the past or the future we are considering. We have no problem in thinking about the 1960s (the TV show *Heartbeat* being an example) without requiring a great deal of historical accuracy. We also have no problem experiencing the future (*Star Trek*, *Stargate*, *Star Wars*) as if it were the present.
- **Paradoxical juxtapositions**. These are odd combinations of things, for example a chemists' shop which sells books and cooking utensils, or a newsagents which sells roast chickens.
- **Fragmentation**. The omnipresence of disjointed and disconnected moments and experiences in life. Markets have become more dynamic, and therefore more fragmented: people are not happy with the same product everybody else owns; the demand is for something new and different.
- **Lack of commitment**. There is a cultural unwillingness to commit to any single idea or project. This is clearly problematical for marketers, since we seek to generate loyalty and involvement with our customers.
- **Decentring of the subject**. Removal of the human being from the central importance he or she had in modern culture, and the increasing acceptance of the potentials of his or her objectification. Individuals are not in control: in marketing, we tend to consider segments and target markets rather than individuals.
- **Reversal of consumption and production**. This is the idea that value is created by consumption, not production. There is some sense in this from a marketer's viewpoint: if a product is a bundle of benefits, it only becomes valuable at the time when the benefits happen, i.e. when the

product is used. Electric drills have no real value if they are simply left in a warehouse until they rot: they do have value when they are making holes. In this sense, consumption actually is production, and vice versa: consumption represents the final stage of the production of benefits.

- **Emphasis on form and style.** Form and style are more important than content in determining meaning and life. The entire fashion industry is based on this concept, as is much of the food industry: frozen ready meals, and even more so a well-presented restaurant meal, are examples of form and style taking precedence over content.

- **Acceptance of disorder and chaos.** The idea that chaos is normal, and that we actually cannot create order out of chaos, is one that might be disturbing to marketing strategists since there is a great deal of planning which will have to be scrapped, but for some marketers the notion of chaos as the norm is a vindication of the idea of hyper-competition (D'Aveni, 1994).

Postmodern marketing offers us a new way of looking at the way the world works, and a new framework for considering marketing problems. It may not provide answers for everything, of course, and as a blueprint for practical marketing it offers very little.

See also: evolution of marketing

REFERENCES

Brown, S. (1997) *Postmodern Marketing Two: Tales.* London: Thomson Learning.
D'Aveni, R. (1994) *Hypercompetition.* New York: The Free Press.
Firat, A.F. and Schultz, J. (1997) 'From segmentation to fragmentation: Markets and marketing strategy in the post modern era', *European Journal of Marketing,* 31 (3/4): 183–207.

The Marketing Environment

> *The marketing environment comprises all those elements of the business world that impact on exchange management.*

Businesses do not operate in a vacuum. They operate within a dynamic environment, in which competitors, customers, government, suppliers and indeed everyone else are each working to their own agendas, doing things that upset carefully laid plans and cause disruption to strategies.

From a marketing viewpoint, managing the exchange process between the firm and its customers comes highest on the list of priorities, but it would be impossible to carry out this function without considering the effects of customer-based decisions on the other stakeholders involved. More importantly, marketers need to recruit the other stakeholders to the cause of meeting customer needs.

The degree to which the environment can be controlled, and the degree to which the environment controls the business, depends in part on the nature of the environment and in part on the nature of the business. Some environmental factors are easily controlled by managers within the firm, whereas others cannot be changed and must therefore be accommodated in decision-making. In general, the larger the firm, the greater the control over its environment: on the other hand, large firms often find it difficult to adapt to sudden environmental changes in the way that a small firm might.

The environment is generally divided into the macro environment and the micro environment. The macro environment consists of all the factors that would affect every firm in the same industry: the economy, government policy, the ecology, the social and cultural environment. The micro environment comprises those factors that only affect the firm: customers, competitors, technology and industry factors, and internal factors such as employees, corporate culture and resource constraints.

The economic environment is essentially about the level of demand in the country, or in the world in the case of a global company. National economies usually follow the boom-and-bust cycle, going into recession (when production and demand fall) every seven or eight years, followed by a boom period when demand grows again. Sometimes countries might avoid this (the UK managed to go from 1992 right into the twenty-first century without a recession, for example), but this is not normal. Recession is defined as a period of two successive quarters when demand shrinks, and it may or may not have serious consequences for firms. Some businesses, notably those dealing in high-ticket products such as cars and household machines such as dishwashers, find that times are hard during recessions, whereas businesses such as breweries and distilleries find that business stays much the same, or even picks up as people feel the need to give themselves a treat.

In most cases recessions only last a few months (although in the 1930s the world economy went into free fall and was only rescued by the Second World War). The issue for marketers is that governments see it as their role to try to prevent recessions, and consequently they will take action that may affect marketing plans. As inflation increases (i.e. prices begin to rise) governments will tend to raise interest rates, which has a limiting effect on consumer spending, and in turn lowers prices. As the economy slows down, governments tend to lower interest rates to stimulate demand. There are many more effects and issues to consider, so marketers are sometimes taken by surprise by government actions, and of course problems elsewhere in the world can seriously affect business in the domestic market – rises and falls in the value of the US dollar, for example, cause international problems because so many raw materials are priced in dollars in international markets.

The socio-cultural environment divides into four main categories, from a marketing viewpoint:

1 **Demographic forces**. As the population shifts in terms of age, wealth, education level and so forth people's needs also change.
2 **Culture**. This is relatively stable over time, but in an international context companies must take account of differences in beliefs, behaviours, customs, language and so forth.

3 **Social responsibility and ethics**. Ethical beliefs derive in part from culture, but ethical beliefs about how firms should conduct themselves clearly affect what marketers can and cannot do.

4 **Consumerism**. This is the shift of power away from companies and towards consumers.

Each of these categories has strong implications for marketing, but since each category affects every other category the solutions are far from simple.

The political and legal environment affects businesses in two main ways: first, governments pass laws that affect business, and second, the prevailing government sets the general tone of behaviour for the country as a whole (although in a democracy it might be argued that the mood of the country decides which party is elected).

The political environment includes the regulatory environment, whether such regulation comes directly from the government or from industry-based bodies. Some examples of government controls in business are as follows:

- **Patent legislation**. Governments set the rules about what may and may not be patented, and for how long. In some industries intellectual property accounts for more or less the whole of the firm's assets (Microsoft and Coca-Cola being examples). Changes in patent (and copyright) law can have profound effects, removing or adding protection to company products and brands.

- **Taxation**. Apart from the general taxation regime on corporations, governments often impose selective taxation on specific products in order to manage demand and raise revenue. In recent years changes in the classification of different products in respect of VAT has had a marked effect on some firms, and in the international context such taxes distort markets: the 'booze cruises' so popular with UK citizens show what happens when different tax regimes operate on different sides of international borders.

- **Safety regulations**. Products need to conform to national safety regulations. Within the European Union many attempts have been made to co-ordinate the wildly differing safety laws in the member states, but results have been poor: the current view is that a product that is legal in one member state is legal throughout the EU, except in cases where human or animal life is threatened.

- **Contract law.** Governments can, and do, amend contract law although much contract law is developed through the decisions of law courts.
- **Consumer protection legislation.** Apart from contract law, mentioned above, governments often enact legislation designed to protect consumers. In the UK there are several hundred laws relating to consumer protection, covering everything from credit agreements to the quality of goods sold.
- **Control of opening hours.** In England and Wales the opening hours of retail shops are only limited on Sundays, when shops may open for six hours only (with exemptions for small businesses). In other countries tougher restrictions apply.

A change in the political nature of the government can make considerable changes in the general tenor of the law. Left-wing governments traditionally increase the number of laws and restrictions on businesses (taking the hand of government approach to ethics mentioned earlier), whereas right-wing governments tend to reduce restrictions on business (taking the invisible hand approach).

Local government and supra-national bodies such as the European Union, Mercosur (in South America) and NAFTA (in North America) can also impose regulations. The EU has, in recent years, been trying to co-ordinate business law throughout the member states, but this endeavour (never easy in the first place) has received a major setback with the accession of ten new member states in 2005. This has meant that ten new legal systems will need to be considered, some of which are relatively new and untried: in the Baltic States, for example, there was virtually no commercial law under Communist rule, so their own business law only dates from 1992 or thereabouts.

The macro environment is difficult to influence, and impossible to control. Only the largest firms are able to influenced government to any extent, and changing cultural or social factors is well beyond the capabilities of any one firm, apart from the faint (and unpredictable) possibility of developing a product that has a dramatic social effect, such as the Internet or the automobile.

The micro environment is a different story. Here marketers can, and do, influence the situation. The micro environment comprises those elements of the environment that impinge on the firm and sometimes its industry, but do not affect all firms in all industries. The micro environment is composed of the following elements:

- **The competition**. In general, the competition is limited to firms providing similar solutions to the same customer problem.
- **Technology**. Some technological changes will leave the company stranded as its products are rendered obsolete, whereas other changes might offer opportunities.
- **Industry structure and power relationships**. This may be related to competition, but equally encompasses supply chains and strategic alliances between firms.
- **Customers**. The pool of customers, the nature of them, the different segments of the market made up of people with slightly different needs, all affect the firm.

Finally, the firm has an internal environment made up of staff relationships, corporate culture and resource constraints. These issues decide everything the firm is able to do, since they impose the limits on decisions that restrict activities. Corporate culture can be developed by managers, but staff relationships and resource constraints are usually a 'given' and are hard to change in the short term. If all goes well, the company's resources will increase and staff relationships can be fostered over time to produce a good working environment, but ultimately companies have to accept much of the internal environment as fixed.

Staff relationships are governed by the formal organisation structure (as shown on the organisation chart) and by the informal structure. The informal structure is composed of the many friendships that people strike up with work colleagues in the course of meeting at the photocopier, going for lunch together, sharing a lift home, and so forth. The informal structure has little or nothing to do with the organisation chart, but it is very powerful in the running of the organisation since it cuts across normal lines of communication, and has the power of social conformity behind it. It provides a degree of flexibility in the organisation, and is the source of goodwill – problems that the official organisation has not envisaged can be solved through the internal network, by asking a favour from a friend. Managers should encourage the informal network to develop, since it injects valuable flexibility into the firm, in a changing world.

See also: strategic planning, marketing research, marketing audit

Marketing Research

Marketing research is the process of finding out about the market in which the firm hopes to succeed, and assessing all aspects of the firm's marketing strategies and tactics.

There is considerable debate about the difference between market research and marketing research, but the basic difference is that market research is concerned with investigating markets (customers, consumers, distribution, etc.) whereas marketing research is concerned with investigating any issues related to marketing (consumer behaviour, advertising effectiveness, salesforce effectiveness, etc. as well as everything contained in market research). Marketing research therefore encompasses market research.

Marketing research breaks down into several separate components, as follows:

1   **Customer research**. This is concerned with the motivation and behaviour of customers, their geographic and demographic spread, their number and spending power and their creditworthiness. It is predominantly used for segmentation and targeting purposes, but is also useful for predicting trends and developing new products.
2   **Advertising research**. This is used to measure the success (or otherwise) of advertising campaigns. The intention is to gain information about which media are most effective, which advertisements are most effective, and which messages reach through to customers best. Advertising research involves the perceptions of customers, so it overlaps considerably with customer research.
3   **Product research**. New products and new product ideas need to be tested on customers, sometimes at the concept stage and sometimes as prototypes. Product research provides information on which features and benefits most appeal to customers, and can also provide information on competitors' products. Packaging is another aspect of

product research, since packaging provides some of the benefits of the product itself: issues here include the extent to which the product is protected from the environment and vice versa, and the degree to which the design of the packaging appeals to distributors such as warehouses and retailers as well as consumers.

4 **Distribution research.** This is concerned with finding the most effective distribution channels. The researchers will be looking for retailers who already deal with the firm's target market, and wholesalers who deal with the appropriate retailers.

5 **Sales research.** Sales research helps to assess the effectiveness of individual salespeople, of different sales techniques and of different sales management methods. It is also useful in designing sales territories to ensure that they are of equal potential: this goes beyond geographical size, it also means including factors such as number of potential customers, distances to travel within the territory and overall wealth of the region.

6 **Environment research.** Scanning the environment for potential threats and opportunities is an ongoing process for most firms. Environment research looks at the social, political, economic and technological factors that might affect the firm and its brands in the future.

Research falls into two main categories: primary research, which is original research carried out for a specific purpose, and secondary research, which is research carried out by someone else for another purpose. Essentially, secondary research is second-hand research: it is published material, sometimes commercially produced, which is available either free or in exchange for a fee. Researchers should always start with secondary research, since it is invariably cheaper than carrying out original research, and may well contain most or all of the answers the researcher is looking for. At the very least it will help inform the primary research, and will probably cut back dramatically on what needs to be researched.

Secondary sources include newspapers, journals, websites, published research, books, academic journals, government reports, commercial research, EU reports and research conducted by trade associations. Internally generated information such as sales records, delivery records, remittance records and so forth can prove valuable. Many firms keep several separate sets of information on customers: salespeople may have records about which customers are difficult to sell to, the finance department might record which customers are bad payers, the shipping department might have records of preferred delivery dates, and so forth. Combining these pieces of data will almost certainly reveal new insights as to which customers are the best to retain, and probably provide guidelines as to which customers should be recruited in future.

Primary data can be collected in several ways, but they broadly divide into quantitative and qualitative methods. Quantitative methods are those in which the results can be expressed in numbers, for example questionnaire surveys, interview surveys, direct observation, test marketing, or panel studies. Questionnaire surveys are probably what most people think of when they think of market research. Questionnaires can either be self-administered, in other words the individual fills in the questionnaire unaided, or they can be conducted by a researcher. Self-completion questionnaires can be sent through the post or by e-mail, which may reduce costs, but they are notoriously difficult to design and usually have low response rates. Interview surveys overcome these problems to an extent, since the interviewer can clarify any points that are unclear, and response rates are usually higher since people find it harder to ignore a person standing in front of them. Observation involves watching what people do and counting the number who behave in a specific way (for example picking up a sample, or looking at a billboard). Test marketing means offering the product within a specific part of the market so that the firm can judge customer responses. Finally, a panel study uses a number of people who have previously been recruited (and are usually paid for their trouble) to report on their buying behaviour. This has the advantage that a large number of products can be studied: it is an economical method of carrying out research, and is often used by commercial marketing research companies.

Qualitative results cannot be expressed numerically, but qualitative research gives insights into consumers' motivations and attitudes. While quantitative research is good for telling what is happening, qualitative research is best for telling why it happened. There are several techniques for qualitative studies. Focus groups, in which between four and eight people are invited to sit around a table and discuss the subject of the research, can often give useful insights as people 'spark' off each other and generate responses that might otherwise not have been available. In-depth interviews with individuals, conducted by a researcher, can drill down to deeply hidden attitudes and motivations, while projective techniques such as the thematic apperception test (in which people are asked to fill in speech bubbles in a cartoon) can reveal secret attitudes. In each case, transcripts of the interviews and focus groups need to be made to enable deep analysis of every word and gesture.

Whichever methods are used, sampling is important. Obviously researchers would be unable to question every possible buyer of the firm's products, so the usual routine is to select a representative group from among the full population. The difficulty lies in ensuring that the selected group really is representative: obtaining a truly random sample is virtually impossible, so researchers usually use non-probability sampling such as quota sampling (in which the researcher starts with knowledge of how the population divides up and seeks out people from each segment), convenience sampling (in which the researcher simply interviews anyone who is available) and judgement sampling (in which the researcher selects a group of people who are believed to possess the necessary information).

Commercial marketing research is not necessarily as rigorous as academic research, mainly because it has to be carried out quickly. Commercial organisations often have to move fast, and cannot wait for the lengthy processes of academic research to work their way through. This sometimes means that analysis and interpretation are less rigorous than they should be as well – so there is a danger that researchers come up with the answer they were expecting, or an answer that pleases the commissioning company, rather than something that is objectively accurate. Additionally, there are serious questions being asked about whether any research can be truly objective: the researcher's own attitudes and biases contribute to the design of any research programme, and of course may (with the best will in the world) contribute to biasing the results.

With all its failings, though, commercial marketing research is still invaluable in providing insights and information for planning marketing activities. It would be difficult to see how any company could manage without some kind of formal marketing research.

See also: *marketing environment, segmentation, targeting*

The Marketing Audit

> *The marketing audit is the checklist by which managers can develop an overall view of the organisation's current position regarding its marketing activities.*

The marketing audit is a method for assessing the current state of play with the firm's marketing. Like a financial audit, it aims to cover all the firm's marketing activities and develop an overall 'snapshot' of every aspect of the firm's marketing, as one of the first stages in developing a strategy. In simple terms, the audit tells us where we are now, so that we can plan on where we want to be and how to get there.

The audit is shown in Table 1.1 below. Working through each area in turn is a useful exercise for marketers, because it helps to focus attention on the important aspects of what the firm is currently doing, and often flags up weaker or neglected areas.

The audit begins with broad themes: the marketing environment audit, the marketing strategy audit, the marketing organisation audit, the marketing systems audit, the marketing productivity audit and the marketing function audit. These broad areas are then broken down into specifics, some of which of course may not be relevant to the firm's particular circumstances.

The audit should be carried out on a fairly regular basis: how frequently will depend on the volatility of the firm's business environment and on the frequency of the planning cycle. The audit appears at first to be a simple matter of ticking boxes, but in fact it requires considerable effort in collecting information, and also considerable care and judgement in analysis. The amount of time and effort involved will need to be balanced against the value of frequent updates of the audit – the more frequent the update, the more effort needs to go into the process, and consequently the less time and energy there is available for day-to-day marketing tasks.

There are of course problems with the marketing audit. First, staff may be reluctant to commit themselves in writing to some aspects of the

Table 1.1 The marketing audit

Main areas	Subsections	Issues to be addressed
Marketing environment audit Macro environment	Economic–demographic	Inflation, materials supply and shortages, unemployment, credit availability, forecast trends in population structure
	Technological	Changes in product and process technology, generic substitutes to replace products
	Political–legal	Proposed laws, national and local government actions
	Cultural	Attitude changes in the population as a whole, changes in lifestyles and values
	Ecological	Cost and availability of natural resources, public concerns about pollution and conservation
Task environment	Markets	Market size, growth, geographical distribution, profits; changes in market segment sizes and opportunities
	Customers	Attitudes towards the company and competitors, decision-making processes, evolving needs and wants
	Competitors	Objectives and strategies of competitors, identifying competitors, trends in future competition
	Distribution and dealers	Main trade channels, efficiency levels of trade channels
	Suppliers	Availability of key resources, trends in patterns of selling
	Facilitators and marketing firms	Cost and availability of transport, finance and warehousing; effectiveness of advertising (and other) agencies
	Publics	Opportunity areas, effectiveness of PR activities
Marketing strategy audit	Business mission	Clear focus, attainability
	Marketing objectives and goals	Corporate and marketing objectives clearly stated, appropriateness of marketing objectives
	Strategy	Core marketing strategy, budgeting of resources, allocation of resources
Marketing organisation audit	Formal structure	Seniority of marketing management, structure of responsibilities

(Continued)

Table 1.1   (Continued)

Main areas	Subsections	Issues to be addressed
	Functional efficiency	Communications systems, product management systems, training of personnel
	Interface efficiency	Connections between marketing and other business functions
Marketing systems audit	Marketing information system	Accuracy and sufficiency of information, generation and use of market research
	Marketing planning system	Effectiveness, forecasting, setting of targets
	Marketing control system	Control procedures, periodic analysis of profitability and costs
	New product development system	Gathering and screening of ideas, business analysis, pre-launch product and market testing
Marketing productivity audit	Profitability analysis	Profitability of each product, market, territory and distribution channel. Entry and exit of segments
	Cost-effectiveness analysis	Costs and benefits of marketing activities
Marketing function audits	Products	Product portfolio: what to keep, what to drop, what to add, what to improve
	Price	Pricing objectives, policies and strategies. Customer attitudes. Price promotions
	Distribution	Adequacy of market coverage. Effectiveness of channel members. Switching channels
	Advertising, sales promotion, PR	Suitability of objectives. Effectiveness of execution format. Method of determining the budget. Media selection. Staffing levels and abilities
	Salesforce	Adequate size to achieve objectives. Territory organisation. Remuneration methods and levels. Morale. Setting quotas and targets

Source: Adapted from *Principles of Marketing*, 3rd edition, Kotler, Armstrong, Saunders and Wong, Pearson Education Limited © Pearson Education Limited 2002.

analysis, and may therefore either shade their reports to put themselves in a favourable light, or may tailor their activities to fit the requirements of the audit rather than the needs of the firm. Second, busy people may not be prepared to spend sufficient time on the process and may therefore simply write down the first thing they think of, on the assumption that the audit is simply a paper exercise. Third, junior executives might put information in the audit which will provoke a response from management that is favourable to themselves. Fourth, the analysis of the data is not always entirely objective – managers may themselves want to appear in a good light, and may therefore (perhaps unconsciously) bias their reading of the data.

To overcome these shortcomings, managers need to generate a 'no-blame' culture, something that is difficult to achieve in the commercial world, or indeed anywhere. Alternatively, different sources could be used for generating the same, or similar, information in order to triangulate on the true situation. This of course adds to the amount of work needed to generate a true picture of what is happening. A third alternative would be to allow each manager to conduct and analyse his or her own part of the audit without being required to pass the results on to anybody further up the organisation. This has the advantage of maintaining at least some degree of objectivity (by removing the office politics) but does not allow anyone to have the whole picture, which is of course part of the purpose of the audit.

A final problem with the marketing audit is that, by the time the data have been collected and analysed, the world has usually moved on considerably and the actual position is somewhat different from what appears in the audit. The true value of the audit is probably therefore that it forces managers to consider in some detail what they are doing and what they might do better. As General Eisenhower famously said, 'Plans are nothing. Planning is everything.'

See also: strategic planning, marketing planning

Competitive Advantage

> *Competitive advantage is the outcome of effective strategy whereby the organisation offers something that competitors are unable to match.*

Strategy is concerned with competitive advantage, and for marketers the obvious corollary is to look for competitive advantage in the marketplace. Strategic planning is intended to create a 'road map' for the company in achieving the organisation's objectives.

Creating competitive advantages means developing some kind of competence within the firm which will enable it to carve out a market for itself against competition from other firms. There are (broadly) four types of competition, as shown in Box 1.1.

Box 1.1 Types of competition

Monopoly   One company controls the market entirely, with no direct competitors. This type of situation is extremely rare, since it almost always results in higher prices and lower efficiency, so it is usually banned by government regulators

Oligopoly   This is a situation where a few very large companies control the market between them, either by colluding with each other (which is illegal) or by a tacit agreement not to anything that would upset the status quo (e.g. start a price war)

Pure competition   A market in which all the players have perfect knowledge, and no single buyer or seller has the power to influence the market. Again, this is rare: the international money markets are one example, but there are few if any consumer markets that operate this way

Monopolistic competition   This is the commonest form of competitive structure, in which one or two large companies have the lion's share of the market, but smaller companies do exist alongside them and can compete effectively

Remaining competitive within a monopolistic competition environment is the challenge facing most firms. There are four basic competitive positions available: market follower, market challenger, market nicher and, of course, market leader.

The **market leader's** position is always to be defending against challengers, but if the firm is to grow it has only two basic alternatives. First, the leader can try to win still more customers away from its smaller rivals (an action that might attract the attention of government regulators). This approach is likely to prove difficult as the smaller competitors fight back. Second, the large firm might decide to expand the overall market. Although this will also help the small firms, it may prove easier to attract new customers into the market than to steal customers from competitors. The objective of the exercise, from the market leader's viewpoint, is to run a successful business, not to out-compete smaller firms. Market leaders can also seek to improve profitability by cutting costs, negotiating strongly with suppliers, or seeking greater economies of scale.

Market challengers seek to increase their share of the market, usually by aggressive competitive tactics aimed at the market leader. Attacking the market leader is risky, since the leader not only has the most to lose but probably also has the most resources, but there is of course the most to gain from a successful attack. Attacking the market followers is probably easier, but the gains are less and the firm might still attract attention from the market leader, since it is of course difficult to acquire customers from only one source – the market leader is bound to lose some customers as well. Market challenger strategies are as shown in Box 1.2.

Box 1.2   Challenger strategies

Frontal attack   The challenger matches the leader's efforts across the full range of products, attacking the leader's strengths rather than its weaknesses. In these circumstances, the company with the greatest resources usually wins, because this strategy leads to a war of attrition. It is usually only appropriate for large firms entering a foreign market, as domestic sales can help subsidise the cost of the 'war'

Flanking attack   Here the competitor concentrates on the leader's weaknesses rather than its strengths. By seeking out a part of the leader's business that is

(Continued)

(Continued)

being poorly served, or could be served better, the challenger often manages to capture a segment without much of a fight. Market leaders will often let a marginal segment go rather than enter into a costly battle

Encirclement attack   This strategy involves attacking from several directions at once. This strategy requires the attacker to have more resources than the defender, so it usually only works well when entering a foreign market

Bypass attack   The challenger bypasses the market leader entirely and targets new markets. This might mean entering foreign markets that the competitor has not yet targeted, or it might mean using new technology to approach new groups of customers. Since the attack is indirect, retaliation by the market leader is unlikely

Guerrilla attack   The challenger makes occasional attacks on the larger competitor, using different tactics each time in order to confuse the market leader and prevent effective retaliation. The constant switching of tactics prevents the market leader from organising a retaliatory attack

Market followers typically seek to avoid doing anything that will incur the wrath of the market leader. They will allow the market leader to make the most of the investment in developing a new market, then follow on to pick up any segments the leader does not find worth pursuing. The followers gain in terms of reduced risks and costs, and as a result they are often as profitable as the market leaders. They do not run the risk of new product failure (the majority of new products fail in the marketplace) because they learn from the mistakes of the market leader: although the largest share of the market usually goes to the innovator, the costs of innovation are so large that the profits often go to the follower.

Market nichers seek to concentrate on small segments of the market, usually segments that are so small and specialised that the market leaders cannot or will not service them. Competitors are often closed out of the niche because the market nicher develops an intimate knowledge of customer needs in a very specialised area. In addition, the niche is often too small to support more than one company, so there is little or nothing to be gained by trying to capture it from an established nicher. Box 1.3 shows the ways in which nichers can specialise.

Box 1.3 Ways to specialise

End-use specialist The firm specialises in meeting all the needs of one type of end-user. For example, Titleist aims to supply all the needs of golfers

Vertical-level specialist The firm specialises in one level of the production–distribution cycle. For example, Pickford's heavy transport firm specialises in moving heavy machinery and abnormal loads. They not only have the specialist vehicles for doing this, they also have knowledge of procedures for alerting police, closing off roads, removing obstacles and so forth

Specific-customer specialist The firm specialises in supplying one or two much larger firms with specialist services or products. For example, Weber carburettors supply high-performance carburettors to most prestige car manufacturers. It is not worth while for the car manufacturers to produce their own carburettors

Geographical specialist The firm might stay within a small geographical area, as does the London Underground. Another example is Welsh-language publishing, which has virtually no market outside Wales and Argentina

Product or feature specialist These firms specialise in producing a particular product, or one with unique features. This strategy is typical for firms with strong intellectual property rights, such as a patent

Quality-price specialist These firms look for a niche at the bottom or the top of a market, either producing the cheapest, most basic version or (more commonly) supplying the highest-quality product. For example, the market for executive jet aircraft is dominated by Learjet

Service specialist These firms offer services that are not available elsewhere. The Russian Space Agency, for example, is the only organisation offering tourist trips into space at present – although other firms are expected to enter the market in the next few years

Gaining competitive advantage is not always appropriate. Some firms seek to collaborate with competitors, and where this is allowed by competition regulators it can prove extremely profitable. For example, Volkswagen, Ford and Seat collaborate on design of some vehicles (the

Ford Galaxy, Volkswagen Sharan and Seat Alhambra are essentially the same vehicle) but each firm competes for customers.

Competitive advantage, and strategy in general, are usually considered from the viewpoint of warfare, and indeed most of the thinking and almost all of the terminology is derived from warfare. However, in recent years there has been an increasing interest in collaborating with competitors, and that being the case we may see a scenario in future where co-operation rather than conflict becomes the norm.

See also: Porter's competitive strategies, strategic planning, positioning

Porter's Competitive Strategies

> *Porter's competitive strategies seek to explain the generic strategic positions a company can adopt in order to generate competitive advantage.*

Porter (1985) suggests four basic competitive strategies: three of these are potentially winning strategies and the fourth is almost invariably a losing strategy:

1 **Overall cost leadership**. A company that minimises its costs can either reduce its prices or increase its profitability, thus obtaining a competitive advantage over other companies. Minimising costs may be a result of developing efficient systems, it may be a result of negotiating better supply prices, or it may mean moving production to lower-cost countries.

2 **Differentiation**. Companies that are able to offer products which their customers perceive as significantly different from competing

products are able to charge premium prices (provided, of course, that the customers believe the differences make the product better). Differentiation can be achieved in two ways: first, by creating real differences in the features and benefits the product offers, and second by creating strong promotional messages that publicise the differences and increase their importance to potential buyers. Both these routes absorb resources, so managers need to be sure that customers will be prepared to pay more for the differentiated product, at least enough to cover the extra costs.

3 **Focus**. Companies following this strategy concentrate on a few market segments rather than trying to compete in the whole market. Often firms concentrate on exclusive markets: the market for luxury yachts falls into this category. In other cases, firms will focus on people with very specific needs – the market for converting vehicles for disabled drivers is highly specialised, for example, with only a handful of firms involved.

The fourth, losing, strategy is to try to combine the strategies. This is impossible, because a differentiation strategy requires the company to commit to higher promotional and research costs, meaning that the firm cannot minimise costs. Likewise, combining low cost with focus will not work, because low cost depends on achieving high sales volumes across a very broad market in order to achieve economies of scale in production. Focus and differentiation may combine if the firm operates in several markets, but there are cost implications which may negate any extra profit that might otherwise accrue.

The essence of a successful strategy is to pursue a clear course of action with which customers can identify, so that the firm has a clear competitive position in the minds of the customers. Customers need to decide whether a firm is cheap, or is best at serving its market segment, or is offering the highest specifications, in order to make firm purchasing decisions.

If there is a lack of consensus among managers, this may result in trying to carry out more than one strategy at a time. Lack of consensus can happen at all levels in the organisation, usually as a result of poor communication of the corporate mission. Consensus among managers improves performance at the strategic business unit (SBU) level, especially for differentiation strategies (Homburg et al., 1999) but is less necessary if the firm is pursuing a low-cost strategy. Low-cost strategies are easy to understand, even if disagreements occur elsewhere.

Treacy and Wiersema (1993) provided an alternative to Porter's categorisation of strategies. Their categorisation identifies three strategies aimed at increasing customer value, as follows:

1 **Operational excellence**. Operationally excellent companies provide better value for customers by leading the industry in price and convenience. The firm tries to reduce costs and create an effective and efficient delivery system, in a similar way to the cost leadership approach.
2 **Customer intimacy**. This strategy requires the company to get as close as possible to its customers, usually by precise segmentation. Close relationships with customers are key to this approach, which in turn usually means empowering the grass-roots staff to make decisions when dealing with customers, and also developing very detailed knowledge of customers' needs and wants. Customers of such companies are usually prepared to pay substantial premiums to get exactly what they want, and tend to be loyal to companies who deliver exemplary service.
3 **Product leadership**. This approach means offering leading-edge, state-of-the-art products and services, aimed at making other products (including the company's own products) obsolete as quickly as possible. Companies following this strategy must be prepared to accept large R&D expenditure as part of the cost, as well as developing systems for getting new products to market as quickly as possible. Staff innovation programmes, and reward schemes based on innovation, are also likely to be needed. Examples of companies that seek product leadership are 3M and Sony, both of which have vigorous new product development systems and substantial rewards for innovative staff.

Treacy and Wiersema's categories are not mutually exclusive, unlike Porter's categorisation. It is perfectly feasible to pursue operational excellence and product leadership, for example.

In practice, senior managers will usually decide what the organisation should and should not be doing and strategy will develop from there: managers may not consciously decide to categorise the strategy according to either of these models. The categories are the result of observing reality, and are not necessarily intended to be prescriptive.

See also: competitive advantage, strategic planning

REFERENCES

Homburg, C., Krowmer, H. and Workman, J.P. (1999) 'Strategic concensus and performance: The role of strategy type and market-related dynamism', *Strategic Management Journal*, 20 (4): 339–57.

Porter, M.E. (1985) *Competitive Advantage*. New York: Free Press.

Treacy, M. and Wiersema, F. (1993) 'Customer intimacy and other value disciplines', *Harvard Business Review*, Jan–Feb, pp. 84–93.

Strategic Planning

> **Strategic marketing planning is the process of formulating corporate objectives and ideals, and developing approaches to achieving those objectives through marketing activities.**

The idea that marketing has a strategic role in running any successful business is deeply embedded in marketing thought. That being the case, marketing has the same need for strategic planning as has any other aspect of strategy, and for the market-orientated company, the marketing strategy is identical to the corporate strategy anyway.

Figure 1.5 shows the levels of strategy in the firm. Marketing may find itself at any or all of the levels, although in many businesses it only occupies a functional level or at most a business level. In other words, marketing is frequently in a subordinate position to the corporate strategy, and is only regarded as a functional device for achieving corporate objectives.

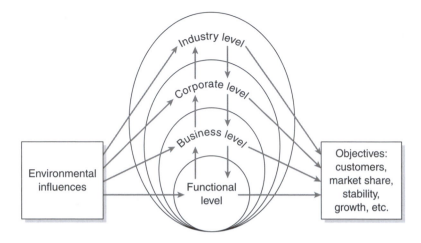

Figure 1.5 *Levels of strategy*

There are six dimensions of strategy (Hax, 1990):

1 Strategy as a coherent, unifying and integrative pattern of decision.
2 Strategy as a means of establishing an organisation's purpose in terms of its long-term objectives.
3 Strategy as a definition of the firm's competitive domain.
4 Strategy as a response to external opportunities and threats, and internal strengths and weaknesses.
5 Strategy as a logical system for differentiating management tasks at corporate, business and functional levels.
6 Strategy as a definition of the economic and non-economic contribution the firm intends to make to its stakeholders.

Ultimately, strategy is what binds an organisation together and gives it direction.

There is no single method for creating strategic plans: if there were, then all companies would end up with much the same strategic plan, which would of course mean that there would be no differentiation between companies. There is a view that planning is cyclical in nature, as shown in Figure 1.6.

In the cycle, strategy is translated into tactics which are implemented, and the evaluation of these tactics is fed back into the strategic planning stage to inform the new stage of planning. The plan is intended to create

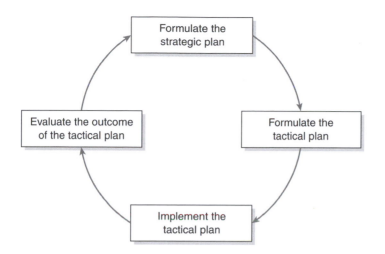

Figure 1.6 *Cyclical nature of planning*

a 'road map' for achieving the organisation's objectives. In most cases this means creating some kind of competitive advantage: corporate objectives may or may not be linked to profitability, since profit is frequently seen only as the means for corporate survival: in other words, profit allows us to stay in the game, but the real objectives lie elsewhere.

In general there are three approaches to planning. The **fully planned approach** details future plans down to the last detail. At the other extreme, the **adaptive approach** means that the organisation changes its strategy and tactics as circumstances dictate, while still maintaining the same general aims and ideals. This is most appropriate in conditions of rapid change. The third model is the **incremental approach**, in which an overall plan is in place, but there is sufficient looseness to accommodate changes if the marketing environment changes unexpectedly. Choice of approach is dictated partly by industry conditions (a volatile industry suggests the adaptive approach, a stable industry allows for the fully planned approach) and partly by the predilections of the corporate founders.

Setting objectives is usually the first stage in planning. There are only three basic marketing objectives (MacKay, 1972). These are:

1 Enlarge the market.
2 Increase share of the existing market.
3 Improve profitability within the existing market share.

According to McDonald (1984), we should move from the general to the particular, from the broad to the narrow, and from the long-term to the short-term. In this way objectives become more focused, and therefore more attainable. A major difficulty with objective-setting is that every problem impinges on every other problem.

Market strategies, whatever their level in the organisation, fall into specific categories. **Market scope strategies** are about coverage of the market, and fall into three categories: single-market strategies, in which the firm devotes all its resources to a single segment; multi-market strategies, in which the firm seeks to serve several segments; and total-market strategies, in which the firm seek to serve every segment of its chosen market.

Market geography strategies concentrate the firm's resources in a single geographic area. Sometimes this can apply to large businesses (the London Underground is an example) but it is often associated with small, local businesses. Regional-market strategy means that the firm operates within distinct geographical boundaries, but these go beyond the local area. This has the advantage that it is easier to identify the brand with a region than with an entire country, or a global market. National-market strategy might be adopted as the firm outgrows its local area, but even within relatively small countries like the UK or Spain cultural differences between different regions of the country can create problems for marketers: simply dealing with Catalan, Basque or Welsh-language issues can be enough to throw the planning off course.

Marketing strategies might also be considered in terms of the **timing** of market entry. First-in marketers gain the advantage of gaining a lead on competitors, but this carries the major risk of possible failure in the market. Early-entry strategy means that much of the risk has already been taken by the first-in company: in most cases, early-entry companies were actually planning to be first in, but were beaten by a competitor. Laggard-entry strategy means entering the market when the basic product is in the maturity phase. This is the lowest risk strategy, and the chances of failure are extremely low (Calentone and Cooper, 1981), but of course the corresponding gains are likely to be lower as well.

Market-dilution strategies are ways of removing the firm from markets that are no longer viable, or do not fit the company's long-term strategy. Demarketing means reducing the marketing effort so that the customers eventually leave: this has the advantage of minimising costs while still extracting the last of the business. Pruning of markets means deliberately closing down operations in those markets, or perhaps selling them to competitors. Key-market strategy is the corollary of pruning: it means diverting resources to the key markets, and losing the peripheral segments. Harvesting strategy means cutting investment in a given brand or market, and treating it as a cash cow. This is a common step when a product is reaching the decline stage of the product life cycle.

This type of careful planning may not be appropriate at all. Whittington (2001) questions the 'toolbox' approach to strategic planning, suggesting that there are four generic approaches to strategy, as shown in Box 1.4.

Box 1.4   Generic approaches to strategy

Classical   Relies on rational planning methods, using environmental analysis as the basis for decision-making and planning for the long term

Evolutionary   Assumes that only the fittest will survive: correct strategies will result from adapting to the environment, and ad hoc solutions are used in response to environmental pressures. Evolutionary strategic thought is about accommodating to the law of the jungle: long-term planning is therefore not feasible

Processualist   Strategy accommodates to the fallible processes of both organisations and markets. Strategy is therefore a bottom-up process, coming from the exigencies of the situations faced by the firm

Systemic   The ends and means of strategy are linked to the cultures and powers of the local social systems in which it takes place. Companies therefore follow policies that are predicated by their local social constraints rather than by strict business considerations

---

Classicists say that strategy is rational, and that a strategic plan can be developed and adhered to. Evolutionists believe that the business environment is too unpredictable for long-range planning, and business is about survival of the fittest. For processualists, strategy is developed as a series of compromises, ad hoc decisions and learning by mistakes, even though the environment is fairly stable. Systemic theorists believe that people can carry out rational plans, but the objectives and outcomes of strategy are embedded in the social systems from which they come.

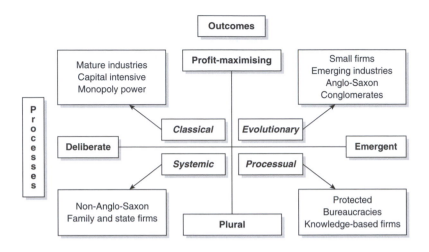

Figure 1.7   *Generic strategies and their implications*

As stated earlier, firms are not always entirely and exclusively profit maximisers. Outcomes can be anywhere on a continuum from profit maximising through to pluralistic outcomes. Likewise, the processes of business can occupy a continuum between deliberate (i.e. thought through) and emergent (i.e. resulting from circumstances) Figure 1.7 shows how the four generic approaches fit along these continua, and the types of business typified by each approach.

The differences between the generic strategies matter a great deal, because each offers a radically different recommendation for managers. For every manager, the planning process starts with a decision as to which theoretical picture of the world best fits with his or her own experiences, attitudes, circumstances and business situation. If the world the manager inhabits is orderly, with sufficient information and capacity to analyse, then the classical paradigm might be most suitable. For managers living in a world that is cut-throat and unpredictable, the evolutionist paradigm is more appropriate.

See also: *competitive advantage, strategic planning*

REFERENCES

Calantone, Roger J. and Cooper, Robert G. (1981) 'New product scenarios: prospects for success', *American Journal of Marketing*, 45: 48–60.

customers and markets

Hax, A.C. (1990) 'Redefining the concept of strategy and the strategic formation process', *Planning Review*, May/June: 34–40.

McDonald M.H.B. (1984) *Marketing Plans*. London: Heinemann.

McKay, E.S. (1972) *The Marketing Mystique*. New York: American Management Association.

Whittington, R. (2001) *What Is Strategy – and Does It Matter?* London: Thomson.

Marketing Planning

> **Marketing planning is the development of strategies and tactics for approaching a group of customers. It is the process of creating an appropriate marketing mix.**

Strategic planning is often likened to drawing up a 'road map' for achieving organisational objectives. This usually means creating a competitive advantage: objectives may or may not be linked to profit, since non-profit organisations also have strategies and seek competitive advantage, and even profit-making organisations often have other objectives as well. Objectives may be linked to growth in market share, or growth in shareholder value, or achieving stability in an unstable market, or any one of many possible outcomes.

The traditional view of planning is that it is cyclical in nature. The outcomes of previous plans and activities are evaluated and used to inform the new strategic planning, so the cycle continues indefinitely. The process may not always be tidy, of course, particularly when the business environment is subject to rapid change.

Given the current emphasis on change in many business environments, planning may seem like a futile exercise. Plans are likely to be upset by technological changes, by competitor activity, or by changes in legislation almost without any warning. On the other hand, without a plan of some sort the organisation may lose its way very rapidly, and

marketing planning

managers have no way of knowing whether their individual actions are helping or hindering if they do not have a clear idea of where the organisation needs to be.

Because of the volatile nature of most business environments, there is no single rule for creating strategic plans. All managers carry out some planning, simply because they must ensure that resources are directed effectively to ensure that objectives are reached. Equally, almost all managers are in the position of needing to manage change, since organisations must respond to changes in the environment. Managers therefore seek to exploit opportunities and avoid threats, by playing to the strengths of the organisation and minimising the effects of its weaknesses.

In general, there are three approaches to planning: first, the **fully planned approach**, in which the organisation's future activities are detailed down to the finest level. Second, the **adaptive model**, which suggests that organisations change the strategy rapidly in the face of environmental changes, and by implication do not plan in detail or very far ahead. This is at the opposite extreme of strategic planning, since it hardly involves planning at all. The third alternative is the **incremental approach**, in which an overall plan is developed but changes are made as circumstances dictate.

In the case of the fully planned approach, planning may be formal, with many of the decisions already made or with established decision-making rules in place, or it may be informal and therefore carried out on an ad hoc basis. Formal strategic planning works best in conditions of stability, where change is slow and where environmental conditions can be predicted fairly accurately.

Some organisations will empower managers throughout the organisation to seek out new opportunities: the organisation is thus characterised by adaptive strategic change. The result of this is an increase in innovation at the business level, with strategy developing from the bottom up: the rationale is that managers who are nearer to the customers (and other stakeholders) can respond much more quickly to changes in stakeholder needs. Adaptation to change will occur much more quickly in such organisations.

Many companies operating in an unstable environment rely on visionary leadership. Visionary leaders have a clear and personal plan of where the organisation is going and what the organisation stands for, and are able to communicate this to the rest of the organisation and its stakeholders.

Such leaders succeed by having a clear grasp of the products, services and activities which the organisation's stakeholders will find acceptable.

Incremental strategic change represents a half-way position between the fully planned system and adaptive change models. The organisation's leadership provides the overall strategy, but sub-strategies emerge from managers throughout the organisation. Managers meet regularly, both formally and informally, to discuss progress and to monitor environmental changes. They will plan new courses of action, and test them in small stages. Incremental strategy works best in organismic organisations in which managers communicate freely and operate on a team basis: hierarchical organisations are less effective for implementing change. An incremental strategy system implies that the organisation must be tolerant of mistakes, which is of course not always the case: Mintzberg (1989) also states that managers must have access to a large amount of appropriate information, and must also be empowered to make the necessary changes in the organisation.

The systems described above are not necessarily mutually exclusive within a large organisation: different divisions within the same organisation may be using different approaches. The management style of the people involved will also affect strategic planning: junior managers may well decide to ignore or pervert the overall strategic plan which has been handed down from the board, perhaps on the grounds that what looks realistic in the boardroom is unworkable in the field. A rapid change in circumstances (for example, a major accident at a corporate factory) may result in the implementation of a predetermined crisis strategy, whereas another sudden crisis (entry of a foreign competitor into the market) may result in the scrapping of a detailed plan. Whatever happens, it is useful to remember that strategic planning does not happen in isolation: no battle plan ever survives first contact with the enemy, and no strategic plan is ever set in concrete. Planning is not a linear process, in other words.

See also: strategic planning

marketing planning

REFERENCE

Mintzberg (1989) *Mintzberg on Management: Inside Our Strange World of Organizations.* New York: Free Press.

> **Globalisation is the process of extending an organisation's activities worldwide, ignoring national boundaries when segmenting markets, sourcing raw materials and components, and carrying out marketing activities.**

International trade goes back a long way. In about 4000 BC a stone axe factory was established in the Langdale Pikes, in the English Lake District. This factory was so successful that axes from it have been found as far away as the South of France – evidence that international trade occurred even before there were true nation-states. Globalisation is the natural extension of international trade.

Globalisation of business has been a hot topic in recent years, with debates and demonstrations about the morality of domination of markets by giant corporations. It has been an important issue in world politics, since fully globalised companies are difficult to control and often act as if they are above government intervention. Protesters have complained about the homogenisation of cultures and the erosion of national diversity as globalised companies enter national markets, often forcing local businesses to close down.

The identification of market segments that cross national boundaries has proved to be a key driver for globalisation. Even if a product only appeals to 0.1% of the world's population, it would still have a market of around six million people worldwide. A company serving such a segment will obtain huge economies of scale in manufacturing, whereas the same segment (on a national basis) might not support development of the product (for example, in the UK the segment would only comprise 60,000 people).

In order to operate in global markets (or indeed in international markets) firms need to adapt the marketing mix to meet local conditions. For most global firms, this means making compromises. A single marketing message means that the firm benefits from economies of scale in its marketing activities, but a single message is extremely unlikely to convey meaning and appeal to the diversity of cultures that exist worldwide.

Figure 1.8 *Forces for globalisation*

The thrust towards globalisation comes from the following factors (see Figure 1.8):

- **Comparative advantage.** Some countries are better-placed to produce certain products than are others – minerals such as oil and aluminium are obvious examples – but some countries develop expertise in service fields. For example, The Netherlands has expertise in building dams and in handling large bodies of water, developed through the construction of its famous dykes.
- **Economies of scale.** For some goods the costs of development are so high that they can only be realistically amortised over very large production runs. For example, products such as electronic games represent a huge cost in terms of research and development – only sales in the millions can justify the outlay, so a world market is essential. Automated production lines mean that manufacturing capacity has increased by orders of magnitude – few modern consumer-goods factories can function efficiently if only serving a domestic market.
- **Trade liberalisation.** For most of the nineteenth century free trade was a major plank in British government policy, because it was recognised that trade always creates wealth. In recent years the idea has received a new

boost with the creation of trading blocs such as the North American Free Trade Area (NAFTA), and the reduction of barriers to trade worldwide as a result of the World Trade Organisation agreements.

- **International product life cycle**. As a product reaches the decline phase in one country, it can be introduced into a new country in order to prolong its life. Due to increased international travel, products frequently cross borders even without the supplier company aiming to internationalise. Because of rapid communications, ideas and designs are disseminated rapidly and copied by manufacturers in other countries.
- **Limited growth in domestic markets**. Most companies aim to grow, but clearly there will come a point at which the home market is saturated. Many firms become international because they cannot grow any more in their home markets, and eventually establish themselves as global markets.
- **Technological changes**. Improvements in air transport and telecommunications have made it much easier for firms to trade in other countries. International TV stations such as CNN and MTV have opened up possibilities to advertise to specific global segments (in the case of CNN, the travelling businessman, and in the case of MTV, the international youth market).
- **Global competition**. Even if a firm has no intention of leaving its domestic market, foreign competition will begin to make inroads into its market. Faced with this type of competition, companies often decide to narrow their target in terms of segmentation, but seek similar segments overseas.
- **Access to resources**. Companies that operate internationally not only sell goods overseas, they also access resources overseas. Manufacture can easily be relocated to low-wage countries, and components can be sourced from overseas suppliers. Eventually firms realise that it is equally easy to sell finished product in those markets, provided they can meet the price/quality requirements of the markets.

A growing factor in globalisation is the existence of transnational market segments. These are groups of consumers with similar needs who inhabit different countries. This may occur because of migration (for example the substantial Malaysian and Chinese communities in Australia and British Columbia) or because of similarities of age (as in the world youth market) or because of similarities in lifestyle (the international executive market). It is far from easy to collect detailed information about these segments because each country operates as a separate entity for the collection of statistics. From a conceptual viewpoint, the truly marketing-orientated company that wishes to go international should be looking for global segments rather than dividing up its customers according to country of residence. Mass migrations and foreign travel are having profound effects on the tastes and needs of consumers throughout the world, with ethnic segmentation growing steadily less easy to apply (Jamal, 2003). Country of residence is becoming less and less relevant as time goes by.

Globalising firms might decide on a standardisation strategy, supplying basically the same products, and using the same attitudes, brands and promotion throughout the world, with global segments being identified. Conversely, the firm might decide on a customisation strategy whereby the company adapts its thinking (and marketing) to each new market. The companies that are most likely to seek a standardisation policy are those whose products are not culturally specific, and whose promotions can be readily understood throughout the world.

Globalisation will continue to be a major force in marketing thinking for the foreseeable future, since for large firms it is the only way forward as home markets become saturated and global markets open up. For the smaller firm, too, the existence of the Internet opens up world markets to niche products, an opportunity that cannot be ignored.

See also: *consumerism*

REFERENCE

Jamal, Ahmed (2003) 'Marketing in a multicultural world: the interplay of marketing, ethnicity and consumption', *European Journal of Marketing*, 37 (11): 1599–620.

globalisation

Consumerism

> Consumerism refers to the shift of power away from producers and towards consumers.

Consumerism has been a feature of marketing since the 1950s, when consumer organisations began to come into being: in the UK, the Consumer Association is the biggest organisation that campaigns on behalf of consumers: the organisation publishes the magazine *Which?*, containing member-generated reports on consumer goods, and the CA also acts as a lobbying and pressure group regarding legislation. In the United States, Ralph Nader's exposure of dangerous features of cars gave a strong impetus to the consumer safety movement, eventually resulting in extremely stringent product liability laws.

Consumer organisations have proliferated in recent years, with specialist groups (such as the Timeshare Consumers' Association) dealing with specific products or parts of the market. Besides taking up specific cases where consumers have been harmed or disadvantaged by companies, consumer organisations lobby government to have changes made in the legislation governing marketers. Consumer organisations also frequently carry out product testing, provide information about companies and products, and even 'blacklist' companies that do not conform to reasonable standards of corporate behaviour.

Some companies use consumer organisations as advisers in product development, since this is easier than changing the product later if the organisation discovers a problem with it. Managers should not therefore consider the consumer movement to be a threat to business: rather, consumerism offers an opportunity to gain more information about issues that concern consumers.

Consumer action groups sometimes arise from interaction with a specific product, or as a result of a common problem. Consumer action groups are grass-root movements rather than formal organisations, and range from neighbourhood watch schemes through to voluntary action to campaign against unethical advertising. Such groups may form for a specific campaign and then disband afterwards, or they may develop into a more permanent consumer organisation which operates over an extended or indefinite timescale.

In an ideological sense, consumerism can be seen in five ways (Gabriel and Lang, 2006):

1 **As a moral doctrine in developed countries**. Consumption has replaced the Puritanical ethic of self-denial in most Western countries. It is seen as the route to happiness, freedom, power and the good life generally. The ability to choose and acquire products, and to consume services, is regarded as a right (which is one of the drivers for the welfare state).

2 **As an ideology of conspicuous consumption**. Social and status distinctions are generated by consumption patterns. People define themselves by what they consume rather than by what they produce: religion, work and political inclination are subsumed in the consumption ethic.

3 **As an economic ideology for global development**. The belief that progress means ever-higher standards of living for ever-more people is an ideological 'given' in most countries. Trade, aid and foreign policy are all informed by this ideal.

4 **As a political ideology**. The modern state is both a guarantor of consumer rights and a provider of many services (the UK's National Health Service being one example). Governments seek to encourage choice in consumer goods, while at the same time investing taxpayers' money into providing better services for people to consume: in a welfare state, government also seeks to ensure that even those who (for whatever reason) do not produce anything can still participate in the consumption process.

5 **As a social movement seeking to promote and protect the rights of consumers**. Consumer advocacy dates back to the co-operative movements of the nineteenth century: interestingly, the consumerist movement has now developed something of a split personality as protection for unbridled consumer choice sits alongside a concern for the environment.

What has become known as the Fordist Deal has driven consumerism. The Fordist Deal was the unwritten contract pioneered by Henry Ford whereby workers are 'promised' ever-higher standards of living in exchange for de-skilled and (to an extent) de-humanised labour on production lines. Ford recognised the potential of his workers as possible customers, and believed that cutting wages simply resulted in cutting the number of potential customers. The result of this has been a tendency to equate success and happiness with material wealth (Lebergott, 1993), and hence to move consumption from being an elite occupation to one that applies to everyone. Governments have become parties to the Fordist Deal, because they try to guarantee full employment and stable currency: they therefore encourage consumption in order to increase employment levels. Some commentators refer to 'the Fordist State' (Hirsch, 1991; Jessop, 2001). Governments have even lost office as a result of failing to keep the promise of higher standards of living for all – the post-war Labour government of the UK was defeated by the Conservatives in 1951 as a direct consequence of their 'austerity' policy, which was swept away by the new government in favour of a consumer-led boom (Hennessy, 1992).

A central feature of consumerism is the separation of production and the circulation of products (often in a glamourised way). Consumers are, of course, the same people who produce goods, despite increased automation, but they will often prefer not to be reminded of the production process, and since the products each individual is involved in producing only represent a tiny proportion of the goods he or she consumes, there is little link between production and consumption.

Consumerism has a global dimension in that it shapes international trade, and even has an influence on war and peace (wars fought to protect supplies of raw materials such as oil are prime examples).

The mass media and advertising have further fuelled the consumerist ideology by linking products with sign values about happiness, identity, beauty, love and other intangible values. These meanings are attached to commodities in order to persuade people to buy, and although marketers do not have the ability to persuade people to buy things, such advertising certainly has an effect on people's tendency to purchase. This is, of course, the area that is of most interest to marketers.

See also: globalisation

REFERENCES

Gabriel, Y. and Lang, T. (2006) *The Unmanageable Consumer*, Second edition. London: Sage.

Hennessy, P. (1992) *Never Again: Britain 1945–51*. London: Jonathan Cape.

Hirsch, J. (1991) 'Fordism and Post-Fordism: the present crisis and its consequences', in W. Bonefeld and J. Holloway (eds), *Post Fordism and Social Form: A Marxist Debate on the Post-Fordist State*. Houndmills: Macmillan Academic and Professional.

Jessop, B. (2001) *Regulation Theory and the Crisis of Capitalism*. Cheltenham and Northampton, MA: Edward Elgar.

Lebergott, S. (1993) *Pursuing Happiness: American Consumers in the Twentieth Century*. Princeton, NJ: Princeton University Press.

Part 2
The Offer

Product as a Bundle of Benefits

> *The concept of product as a bundle of benefits is the theory which seeks to explain a product from the viewpoint of a consumer.*

Products are what marketers supply in exchange for customers' money. From the producer's viewpoint, a product is the end result of combining factors of production, i.e. labour, raw materials, capital and enterprise, but from a customer's viewpoint the product is defined by the benefits it provides. Since marketing involves seeing everything the firm does from the viewpoint of the customer, marketers define products as bundles of benefits.

A distinction needs to be made here between a feature and a benefit. A product feature is something that describes the product in terms of its physical characteristics. For example, a book might be described as having four-colour printing, end-of-chapter questions, easy-to-read print, boxes on global issues, two case studies per chapter, soft cover and vignettes drawn from real life. This would accurately describe the book, but it would not tell the book purchaser why these features are of any use at all. For features to be converted to benefits, the marketer needs to explain what each feature means. This is illustrated in Table 2.1.

The benefits of the product might be categorised by the customer in different ways. Products provide five different types of benefit: functional, operational, personal, quality and financial. These are described as follows:

1 **Functional benefits.** These relate to the product's capacity for doing what the consumer expects it to do. For example, a stereo system might be judged on its ability to play vinyl as well as CDs and on its power (or loudness) level. The tuner might be judged on whether it can pick up long wave as well as FM.
2 **Operational benefits.** These are similar to functional benefits, but apply specifically to business-to-business markets. Operational benefits are

Table 2.1 Converting features to benefits

Feature		Benefit
Four-colour printing	Which means that ...	The book is attractive
End-of-chapter questions	Which means that ...	The reader can check his or her understanding of the text
Easy-to-read print	Which means that ...	The reader will not get tired or strained reading the book
Boxes on global issues	Which means that ...	The reader gains an insight into how each chapter relates to the global context in which business operates
Two case studies per chapter	Which means that ...	The text is placed in the context of the real world
Soft cover	Which means that ...	The book is lighter to carry and cheaper than a hardback version
Vignettes drawn from real life	Which means that ...	Complex theoretical material is explained in easily understood contexts

those that influence the buyer's production process. For example, the buyer might want to know whether the proposed product will increase profitability, will improve productivity, or will reduce labour costs. Such considerations might apply to some consumer goods, of course – if the new Hoover is better at cleaning the carpet, the time spent doing so will be reduced.

3 **Personal benefits.** In many cases the product provides intangible, psychological benefits to the customer. These may be difficult for the marketer to gauge: for example, a customer who is an amateur musician might buy a specific brand of guitar strings because they provide the best sound, or might buy them because his or her guitar hero is known to use them. Personal benefits come to the fore when people buy prestigious brands, especially when the brand is visible to others (for example, buying an upmarket car).

4 **Quality.** Quality has been defined as the relationship between what someone expects and what they get. It is often judged by corporate

reputation, by examining the materials used in production, or even by looking at the price tag. Quality relates to expected performance – high quality means that customers expect the performance to be perfect, they probably expect the product to be well made and reliable, and they expect to pay a premium price for these benefits. Poor quality means that the product will probably not last long, and will not do a great job, but will be cheap (which may well compensate for the drawbacks).

5   **Financial benefits.** These relate to the investment potential of the product. In some markets these benefits may be very important: holiday homes, timeshare, insurance products, and of course savings accounts are all considered as investments. In others financial benefits might relate to the savings the product will make.

Considering the product as a bundle of benefits has definite advantages to firms when planning promotional campaigns. Advertisers have long understood that ads should sell the benefits, not the features (sell the sizzle, not the sausage, was a common way of expressing this). In some markets this principle seems to have been mislaid, however: much of the computer hardware and peripheral products seem to describe themselves in terms of features without explaining what the features mean. This is not necessarily a problem for a computer enthusiast, who can easily work out what a 30GB hard disc will do, but for the average buyer this jargon needs to be explained. (For those who fall into this category, the term refers to the amount of memory the computer has; 30GB is a medium-sized memory which would hold around 100 of the textbooks mentioned earlier.)

Marketers tend to talk about physical products a great deal, despite the fact that the bulk of expenditure in the Western world is on service products. The idea of a product as a bundle of benefits applies equally to service products, and from the viewpoint of a customer a service might provide much the same benefits as a physical product. For example, if someone wants to buy a special treat for a spouse, they might decide to buy a physical product such as a necklace or a set of golf clubs, or might equally decide to buy a weekend away at a good hotel. Equally, someone in need of a morale boost might buy themselves something nice to wear, or might go to the cinema, or might even buy a train trip to visit an old friend. Service benefits can still be categorised along the same lines as physical goods (functional, operational, personal, quality and financial) and can be regarded as equally valuable.

See also: need satisfaction, added value, service products

Product Anatomy

> *Product anatomy is the analysis of a product according to the different benefits it offers.*

A product can be seen in terms of the benefits it offers to different buyers. Figure 2.1 shows the structure of a product in terms of different layers of benefits offered.

At the centre of the product is the **core product**. This is the basic product, and represents the main benefits for which the product is purchased in the first place. The core product usually provides the same benefits as competing products in the same category, so there is little or no differentiation at this stage. For example, all cars provide transport for people and luggage: these are the core benefits, and that is therefore the core product. Of course, when cars first appeared on the roads they were competing with the horse and carriage, which also supplied the same core benefits, but in a somewhat different way.

The **tangible product** is the design, the specific features, the overall package that communicates the benefits of the core product. In the case of a car, the tangible product would include the styling, the engine, the seating, the amount of boot space and so forth. These are the practical aspects of the product, the way in which the benefits are being delivered. At this point the car begins to look very different from the horse and carriage, even though both deliver the same core benefits.

The **augmented product** represents the extra features and benefits that differentiate the product from others in the same category. This might include (in the case of a car) the cup-holders, radio, air conditioning, air bags and so forth. Equally, the augmented product might include service features such as free or low-cost financing, free servicing, delivery or long-term warranties. The purpose of augmenting the product in this way is to make it stand out from its competitors and to provide benefits that they are unable to match, thus shutting out competition from some segments of the market. For example, when Korean car manufacturer Daewoo entered the UK market, the company offered three-year servicing for the cars. This was an impressive offer which other companies simply could

the offer

66

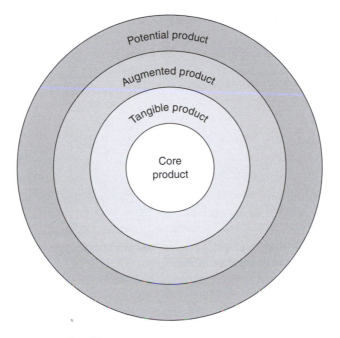

Figure 2.1 *Layers of benefits*

not match: it had the advantage of demonstrating that Daewoo clearly had confidence in the reliability of the cars. Market-leading brands such as BMW, Levi, Zanussi and Red Bull have augmented their products (mainly via intangibles) to the point where their position seems almost unassailable.

The **potential product** represents all that the product might become in the future. Products need to be developed as time goes on, and eventually new models will appear which will include new tangible benefits and will have new augmentations. Because of these potential new benefits, consumers feel happy to associate themselves with the brand: the fact of owning a leading brand is in itself a benefit, even if the potential benefits have not yet materialised and will only do so if the new model is purchased.

All four layers of product provide benefits to the ultimate consumer, but the outer layers all depend on the core product for their definition. The core is the starting point for the entire process, even though the main competitive activities occur in the outer two layers. From a marketer's viewpoint, the key to success lies in understanding which benefits our target customers will want to see in the augmented product and the potential product.

See also: core product, need satisfaction, product as a bundle of benefits

Core Product

> **The core product is the basic group of benefits which all products in the category would be expected to offer.**

Products can be considered as having several levels, each offering differing benefits to their consumers. The core product is the main reason for its existence and purchase, and comprises the benefits that would be considered basic to any product in the same category. For example, the core product benefits of a television set would be entertainment based on broadcast programmes. All television sets would be expected to have this minimum level of function, whatever other features and benefits (stereo sound, teletext etc.) the set might also provide.

From a consumer's viewpoint, the features of the core product form **hygiene factors** (Herzberg, 1959). Hygiene factors are those elements which, if present, do not create any satisfaction or motivation in themselves, but which (if absent) create dissatisfaction and demotivation. The core product acts as a basis for the tangible product (which is the extra benefits that differentiate the product from its competitors) and the augmented product, which also includes peripheral benefits such as after-sales service, helplines or even training in the use of the product.

The core product's basic description and features may need to be adapted over a period of time as consumer expectations shift. As people come to expect more from a product as 'basic', disappointment sets in if the product does not have the required features. For example, in the 1930s windscreens were often sold as an optional extra on cars, and in some cases this practice continued into the 1950s. Radios were not generally regarded as a standard, expected piece of equipment on cars until the 1970s, yet nowadays people might be surprised to find a new car without a radio, CD player and air conditioning fitted as standard. Because the core product includes the term 'in reasonable comfort' the actual features required to achieve this could be almost anything that is offered as standard from all car manufacturers.

Another aspect of the core product is that the features that provide the core benefits might differ dramatically. Taking the example of a car, if the core benefit is to provide transportation for the driver, the passengers and their luggage in reasonable comfort, a light aircraft or a boat might be considered to provide the same benefits. In some parts of the world (the Australian outback, for example) light aircraft are frequently used as transportation for day-to-day tasks such as shopping or visiting friends, and in many island communities (such as the Greek Islands) boats are used for similar purposes. Since core benefit is defined by the consumer, the features that provide it might be seen to be interchangeable.

The basic core product concept, however, is generally used by producers to define how their products differ from competing products within the same category. Having defined the core product, and ensured that it does genuinely meet the basic requirements of any purchaser, whatever remains must be what differentiates the product.

See also: product anatomy

REFERENCE

Herzberg, F. (1959) *The Motivation to Work*. New York: John Wiley & Sons.

Added Value

> Added value is the concept that companies exist to add value to the inputs they receive. The type of value added will dictate the firm's competitive advantage.

Adding value means that the company sells products that are more valuable than those it buys. In some cases the value is added by transforming raw materials or components into something that is more useful, in other cases value is added by applying a service component to a product or group of products.

Value is not necessarily added simply by inputting effort: the right effort needs to be made if value is to be created rather than destroyed, and the amount of value created will vary greatly according to the inputs the company gives. As an analogy, a chef can take ingredients such as herbs, spices, meat and vegetables and create a tasty stew: a great chef, starting with the same ingredients, can create a dish fit for a king: while a bad chef can take already-valuable ingredients and create an inedible mess. The value created from a company's efforts is divided (not necessarily equally) between the company and its customers. Customers always gain by buying from the firm, or they would not do so, and equally the company gains value in the form of profit, which allows it to stay in the game and continue in business.

In marketing terms the added value concept appears in two areas: first, in distribution networks, and second, in product development. In distribution, each intermediary adds value in some way, otherwise they would quickly be excluded from the distribution network. Wholesalers add value for producers in the following ways:

- Carrying out some promotional activities.
- Warehousing, storage and product handling.
- Transport of local and sometimes long-distance shipments.
- Inventory control.
- Credit checking and credit control.
- Pricing and collection of pricing information.
- Channelling information up and down the distribution network.

For retailers, they add the following values:

- Information gathering and dissemination.
- One-stop distribution of a wide range of products from many manufacturers.
- Facilities for buying relatively small quantities.
- Fast deliveries or cash and carry.
- Flexible ordering and supply.
- Bulk breaking – taking large deliveries and breaking them down into manageable quantities.
- Sorting out variable products such as fruit and vegetables into differing qualities.

If wholesalers did not exist, other members of the distribution chain would have to perform these tasks, probably less efficiently and at greater cost. Although some major retailers are big enough to carry out the functions of a wholesaler, the majority of retailers are not in that position – they cannot order goods in sufficient quantities to be economic for a manufacturer. Likewise, retailers provide easy access for consumers to a wide range of products, in a way that would be difficult or impossible for other members of the chain. Consumers are really not in a position to go to each manufacturer within a product category to check quality and prices, and equally the manufacturers are not in a position to supply single items to consumers.

The value added by intermediaries is always greater than the profit margin they add on, otherwise they would be bypassed by other distribution chain members. Therefore, cutting out the middle man (a common idea for reducing prices) would be more likely to raise prices, since the distribution chain would function much less efficiently. For example, a can of tuna moves through perhaps eight or more intermediaries before it arrives in the consumer's food cupboard, yet it only costs pennies. It would clearly cost a lot more if the fishermen in the Pacific had to deliver each tuna chunk to the individual consumer.

The role of added value in product development is also important. Product strategy involves deciding what products to produce, and in particular it involves deciding how the firm's products are going to meet customer needs. Equally, product strategy is concerned with deciding how the firm's products fit with competitive offerings. It is this aspect which involves the concept of added value.

Generic or commodity products are basic products that have all the core benefits of the product. The drawback with producing generic or commodity products is that all other products on the market have the same core benefits, so virtually the only options open to the company if it is to compete effectively are either to compete on price, or to compete on peripheral issues such as delivery. For example, a firm making cement can only compete if it either sells the cement cheaper, or if it offers exemplary delivery services, or possibly technical advice. Competing on price cuts profit margins dramatically, and there is almost always another firm which can produce at an even lower price, or one that is prepared to sell below cost price in order to enter a market. In some cases, Third World and Communist countries are able to sell below the cost of manufacture simply as a way of obtaining hard currencies – which means that full-cost companies in the target countries have no hope of competing on price.

Producing commodity products means competing on price, and thus squeezing profits: adding value means that prices can be raised. Of course, commodity companies have zero research and development costs, low or zero promotional costs and virtually zero re-tooling costs, but these probably do not compensate for the loss of profits caused by price competition.

Levitt (1983) suggested the following hierarchy of product levels (see *product anatomy*, p. 66):

1 **Core or generic level.** This is the basic physical product, or the minimum features and benefits a customer for this type of product would expect. All the products in the category would share these features and benefits.
2 **Expected product.** This is the generic product, plus some extra features that most people would reasonably expect to see.
3 **Augmented product.** These are the features that differentiate the product from competing products in the category.
4 **Potential product.** These are all the benefits that could possibly be wanted by customers. No product would normally have all these features: if it did, it would be impossibly expensive and cumbersome, but the list should still be developed so that the company has a menu of features and benefits to choose from when seeking to differentiate, and in particular when seeking to develop new products.

Adding features from the 'potential product' list should add value for the customer, which should in turn help to differentiate the product. The key issue here is whether the cost of adding the extra features and benefits is greater than the premium the customer is prepared to pay. If it is, then the company will lose money by adding the feature.

Added features should follow the criteria laid down by Doyle (1998):

1 The feature must be important to customers.
2 It should be unique.
3 It must be sustainable in the face of competitive retaliation.
4 It must leave the product marketable at an acceptable price.

The key factor from this list is that the added feature must be important to customers; in fact it should provide a benefit that is valuable to customers, otherwise there is no reason for them to buy it. Clearly different people will place different values on each feature, so the feature must be something which the company's target customers will see as desirable.

In recent years the concept of added value has come under some criticism. For many years manufacturers have added more and more features and benefits to products, seeking to out-do their competitors on adding value to their offerings. Airlines in particular went down this route, offering ever-better in-flight meals, slicker check-in and boarding, more comfortable seats and so forth. This eventually left the way open for low-cost, no-frills airlines to enter the market with commodity products, offering only the core benefits of carrying passengers from one place to another. The result of this was that, at a time when major carriers were losing money or even going bankrupt, the low-cost airlines were carrying record numbers of passengers and making record profits. A similar effect occurred in the US car market during the 1970s, when the majors (Ford and General Motors) were taken by surprise by Japanese companies entering the market with cheap, basic cars that were reliable ways of getting from A to B and not much else.

Clearly there is a balance to be struck. Adding more and more features and benefits is not always going to be effective, but equally staying with just the core product is also unlikely to be a success. Maintaining a clear view of what customers actually value at any one time is core to success, as always in marketing.

See also: new product development

REFERENCES

Doyle, P. (1998) *Marketing Management and Strategy*. London: Prentice Hall.
Levitt, T. (1983) *The Marketing Imagination*. New York: Free Press.

service products

Service Products

Service products are those bundles of benefits that comprise a high level of intangible factors, usually provided by people.

Services are also bundles of benefits, so are products as much as are physical items. For many marketers, the difference between the marketing of services and the marketing of physical goods is negligible, for the following reasons:

- A product is a bundle of benefits. An individual seeking to be cheered up may achieve this by going out for dinner (a service) or by buying a bottle of wine (a physical product). The benefit (an improvement in mood) is basically the same.
- The problem of defining whether a product is a service or a physical product. Most tangible products include a service aspect, and most services include some kind of physical product. In other words, most purchases lie somewhere along a continuum between purely service and purely physical products.
- Consumer orientation means that (as marketers) our focus is on what the consumer thinks, needs and wants, so we should be defining our products in terms of consumer benefit not product characteristics.

There are products where the major part of the cost of the product is the service element, for example, a hairstyle. Here the cost of the raw materials (the shampoo, conditioner, hair tints, perm solution) is only a tiny part of the overall cost of the hairdo. A complete restyle costing a week's wages may only use one-tenth that value in materials: the customer is paying for the time and skill of the stylist, the pampering from the staff of the salon, the ambience and the general feeing of well-being that comes from looking smart and attractive.

The main differences between service products and physical goods are shown in Box 2.1. The risk attached to buying a service is higher (from the consumer's viewpoint) than is the risk of buying a physical product. Physical products are easily returned if they fail to satisfy; it is impossible to return a poor haircut, and unless the standard is very poor, it may even be difficult to avoid paying for it. Even a minor defect in a personal stereo can justify returning the item: an uncomfortable train journey in the company of badly behaved drunks will not result in a refund of the fare.

When choosing a service provider, most people are likely to spend more time on information-gathering, and are more likely to rely on word-of-mouth recommendations than they would when buying a physical product. The intention is to minimize the risks inherent in service purchases. For professional services, people will often want to know about the credentials and experience of the service provider. For example, someone choosing a financial adviser may want to know what experience and qualifications the adviser has, whereas few car buyers would be interested in the qualifications and experience of Renault's designers.

Box 2.1   Factors Distinguishing Services

Services are intangible   Financial advice is more than the paper it is written on; the key benefit (financial security) cannot be touched

Production and consumption often occur at virtually the same time   A music concert happens at the same time as the audience enjoys the performance

Services are perishable   An airline seat is extremely perishable; once the aeroplane takes off, the seat cannot be sold. Services cannot be produced in advance and stockpiled

Services cannot be tried out before buying   It is not usually possible to try the food in a restaurant before deciding whether to order it

Services are variable, even from the same supplier   Sometimes the chef has a bad day, or the waiter is in a bad mood; on the other hand, sometimes the hairdresser has a flash of inspiration that transforms the client's appearance

---

Service purchasing follows a slightly different sequence from purchase of a physical good, as shown in Figure 2.2. Most of the risk attached to buying a physical product is limited to the purchase price, and problems are easily fixed by refunding the money or replacing the product, but services carry additional risks that are more difficult to correct.

- **Consequential losses** arise when a customer loses out as the result of a failed service. For example, a lawyer who makes a major error in arguing a case could lose thousands of pounds for his or her client, or even cause his or her client to be jailed in a criminal case. Service providers usually are careful to explain the risks beforehand, use disclaimers in contracts and carry professional liability insurance. Consumers can sue for consequential losses.

- **Purchase price risk** is the possible loss of the customer's money if he or she buys a service that fails. The usual consumer response is to refuse to pay for the service, so it is advisable for the supplier to check during the service process that everything is satisfactory. This is why waiters often ask diners if their meals are satisfactory, and why car mechanics call customers when they find something serious is wrong with the car. Checking during the service provision not only makes it easier to correct problems early, it also makes it harder for customers to claim that the service went wrong in order to avoid paying.
- **Misunderstanding** is common in service provision because the service usually cannot be tried out in advance. In professional services, professionals such as accountants and lawyers may feel that the customer would not understand the technical details of what is being done, and may therefore not be able to explain properly. This can easily result in post-purchase dissonance and refusal to pay.

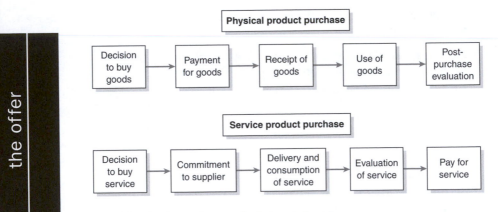

Figure 2.2   *Service purchase* vs. *physical product purchase*

Because consumers are buying a promise, they are more likely to use indirect measures of quality such as price. Diners tend to assume that more expensive restaurants will provide better food and/or service; that expensive hairdressers will provide better hairdos; and that expensive lawyers are more likely to win cases. Once a commitment to a service provider has been made, the consumer is more likely to become involved with the service provider (see the section on involvement). Most of us tend to have favourite restaurants, hairdressers and family solicitors, and in many cases these relationships continue for many years, or even a lifetime. Customers are reluctant to switch bank accounts, even when problems have become apparent; even though customers will readily change brands of breakfast cereal in order to save a few pence, they tend to stay loyal to the same supermarket. This is because the customer knows where everything is kept in the supermarket, understands the store's policy on returned goods, knows which credit cards are acceptable and perhaps even knows some of the staff on the tills.

As a product moves towards the services end of the spectrum, there is more emphasis on people, process and physical evidence (Booms and Bitner, 1981). Because most services involve direct contact between the producer and the consumer, the people delivering the service become part of the overall product: a hairdresser's personality affects the customer experience, whereas the personality of a factory worker does not.

Since the consumer is usually present while the service is being provided, the process becomes as important as outcomes in a service market. Buying an airline ticket online is an extremely convenient process compared with making a visit to a travel agent, for example. Finally, physical evidence is the tangible evidence of the service's quality, and even of its existence. Since service products are usually intangible, the consumer of (say) an insurance policy will need some written evidence of its existence in order to feel confident in the product. Physical evidence can also include the décor, fittings and atmospherics of the shop or office where the service is delivered.

In many ways services can be marketed in similar ways to physical products. In most cases there is no clear demarcation between physical products and services, so the techniques for marketing them will not differ greatly.

See also: *product as a bundle of benefits*

REFERENCE

Booms, B.H. and Bitner, M.J. (1981) 'Marketing strategies and organisation structures for service firms', in J. Donnelly and W.R. George (eds), *Marketing of Services*. Chicago, IL: American Marketing Association.

service products

The Product Life Cycle

> **The product life cycle is the model that seeks to describe and explain the sales of a product from its introduction through to its obsolescence and withdrawal.**

A key concept in product portfolio management is the product life cycle (PLC) (see Figure 2.3). The PLC is based on the assumption that products move through a series of stages from their introduction, passing through a growth stage, followed by a maturity phase in which sales remain stable, through to a decline phase and final withdrawal from the market. Products tend to lose money when they are first introduced: sales are low, marketing costs are high and there no economies of scale in production. Eventually, if the product follows the PLC, its sales improve and it begins to return a profit, but sooner or later the growth in sales will peak out. This is because the market becomes saturated: everyone who will adopt the product has done so, and sales steady out as the product is kept afloat by repeat sales. As alternative products enter the market, or as the product goes out of fashion, it will go into a decline and will eventually cease to have any market.

In fact, the situation is often much more complex than this, so the basic product life cycle (as shown in Figure 2.3) does not always describe what actually happens in practice.

Although the PLC is useful for explaining what happens to products, it suffers from a number of weaknesses. First, there are no time-scales, so the model cannot predict with any accuracy what will happen over a given period of time: for a fashion item, the maturity phase might only last a few months, whereas for a product such as pitta bread the maturity phase has already lasted several thousand years and shows no sign of changing.

Second, marketing activities will affect the shape of the curve. As the product's sales decline, marketers might decide to re-launch the product in a new market, or might run a promotional campaign to revitalise sales, or might decide to concentrate resources on another product in the portfolio and drop the declining product. These alternatives are shown in Figures 2.4 and 2.5.

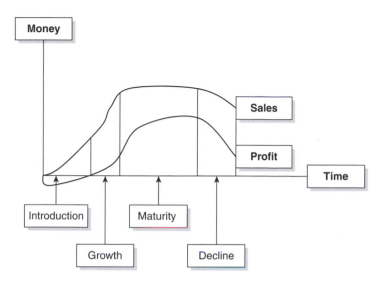

Figure 2.3 *The product life cycle*

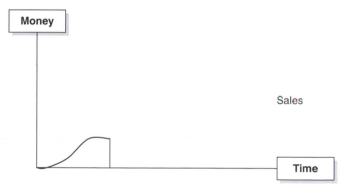

Figure 2.4 *Product dropped shortly after introduction*

Third, some products come back into fashion after a few years of being absent from the market. Recent examples include the Mini Cooper, the Volkswagen Beetle and the yo-yo.

Fourthly, the vast majority of new products fail, but the PLC assumes that all products go through the same general pattern of life. A failed new product might exhibit a lifecycle such as that shown in Figure 2.6, where the product never moves into profit.

Finally, the PLC is not much help in managing the product portfolio because it only looks at one product. Most marketing managers have to

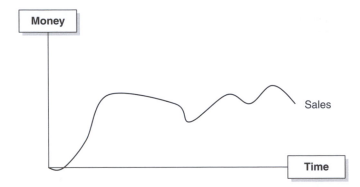

Figure 2.5 *Effects of marketing activities on the product life cycle*

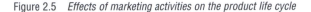
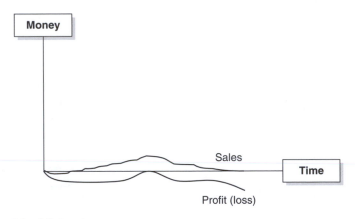

Figure 2.6 *Failed product*

balance the demands of many different products, some of which will need more support, some of which may be doing badly in themselves but which help the sales of other products, and so forth.

Despite these weaknesses, the product life cycle is widely quoted and used in making decisions about marketing tactics. The type of decisions to be made might be as follows:

1 **Introduction phase**. The corporate strategy is likely to be to build the market as quickly as possible, since this is an effective way to estab-lish a large share of the market before competitors can respond. It is likely that the initial product will be a fairly basic model, since the market is new and there will have been little opportunity to improve

it. Promotional effort will concentrate on creating awareness and encouraging trial of the product, because research shows that advertising is more effective in the introduction phase than it is later (Vakratsas and Ambler, 1999). The price may well be high, since the firm needs to recoup development costs and competitors have yet to introduce their own versions of the product. Distribution of the product is unlikely to be comprehensive in this phase of the PLC, since many distributors will not want to risk carrying an unknown product.

2 **Growth.** The main emphasis of the firm's marketing will still be on building the market as quickly as possible, but the promotional thrust will shift from creating awareness towards encouraging repeat purchases and brand preference. The product itself is likely to be available in several different versions by now, and from several different suppliers: the price will have dropped due to competitive pressure, since competitors' development costs will have been considerably lower. Since competitors had an existing product to copy, they can show a profit despite charging a lower price. Distribution will be much wider in the growth phase as distributors become more confident of selling the product.

3 **Maturity.** In the maturity phase the company will seek to maintain market share in the face of increased competition. Promotion is aimed at maintaining brand loyalty and awareness. The price is now at its lowest point, and there will be several versions of the product available in order to meet the needs of different sub-segments of the market. Competitors will be looking to increase market share by the use of aggressive marketing tactics, and distribution is likely to be intensive.

4 **Decline.** In the decline phase, the most likely strategy is to harvest. This means that very little money is spent on promoting or developing the product further, and it is allowed to decline. The company can still reap a profit from the remaining sales because the investment level is now very low. Not all versions of the product will be available at this stage, since the company will be rationalising the range to reduce production costs. The price may be rising in order to make as much as possible from the remaining sales. Distribution will be less widespread as some distributors decide that the declining sales no longer justify carrying the product. Eventually, the product will be eliminated as it will no longer be viable. In fact, most decisions to eliminate products are made on

the basis of intuition and judgement rather than any formal analysis (Greenley and Barus, 1994), as evidenced by the fact that new managers often try to revive the product's fortunes by investing in the brand.

For some companies, it may not be worth investing in new products at all, and in fact there are companies that have produced essentially the same product for many years. These companies do not innovate, and therefore do not have research and development expenditure to find, but they do run the risk of their product being superseded by a superior competitive product. Also, research shows that new products are more successful than sales promotions in producing the following results (Pawels et al., 2004):

- Long-term financial performance and firm value.
- Investor reaction (which grows over time).
- Yielding top-line, bottom-line and stock market benefits.

This in itself means that new products are worth pursuing. The product life cycle provides marketers with a way of thinking about products, and with a set of terminologies for discussing development strategy, but it is not (and is perhaps not intended to be) an accurate predictive tool.

See also: new product development

REFERENCES

Greenley, G.E. and Barus, B.L. (1994) 'A comparative study of product launch and elimination decisions in UK and US companies', *European Journal of Marketing*, 28 (2): 5–29.

Pawels, Koen, Silva-Risso, Jorge, Srinavasan, Shuba and Hanssens, Dominique M. (2004) 'New products, sales promotions and firm value: the case of the automobile industry', *Journal of Marketing*, October, 68 (4): 142–56.

Vakratis, D. and Ambler, T. (1999) 'How advertising works: what do we really know?', *Journal of Marketing*, 63 (Jan): 26–43.

the offer

New Product Development

New product development is the process of creating new benefit offerings for customers.

The product life cycle tells us that, eventually, all products will reach a peak of maturity and go into decline (unfortunately the product life cycle does not provide any time-scales for this process). Since products eventually become obsolete, firms need to develop new ones on a fairly regular basis. Equally, competitors will be trying to develop products that will increase their market share at the expense of other firms, so each firm needs to meet competitive challenges even when the existing products are perfectly acceptable to consumers.

Reactive new product development (NPD) is the approach taken by firms that simply respond to competitive initiatives, rather than responding to customer needs. This is not an unreasonable approach from a strategic viewpoint, since the initiating company is taking all the risks of failure in the market: on the other hand, the reactive company loses first-mover advantage, and therefore may never acquire a large share of the market. Frequently, reactive companies are forced to compete on price, so although the risks are lower, the returns are also correspondingly low. A proactive firm seeks out new ideas, spends more on research and development, and is looking to gain from first-mover advantage. Such firms spend a great deal of money on research and development, and are prepared to accept a high-risk, high-return strategy. Many new products fail to recover their development costs, so the firm needs to do well on the ones that do succeed: however, often the product can be protected by patent (as is the case in the pharmaceutical industry) so there will be a long-term flow of income from the initial investment, and little or no competition.

The task of creating new products is not an exact science. It is therefore difficult to generalise about the process, but a frequently quoted model of the NPD process was given by Crawford (1994), and follows this sequence:

1 **New product planning**. The firm examines its current portfolio, opportunities and threats and decides what kind of new product would best fit in with future strategy.
2 **Idea generation**. Specific ideas for the product are expressed, perhaps through a brainstorming session of the venture team.
3 **Screening and evaluation**. The ideas are checked for feasibility and marketability.
4 **Technical development**. The engineering aspects of the product are investigated, and a prototype is developed.
5 **Market appraisal**. Formal market research is carried out to assess the product's viability in the market.
6 **Launch**. Assuming the market research is positive about the product, the firm puts it into production.

Although all of these stages are likely to be covered in one form or other the methods used may be subjective, or carried out ineffectively. Frequently the somewhat haphazard approach taken by some managers leads to problems following the launch of the product. For example, a full (and objective) market appraisal may not be carried out because the people who are in charge of the project (the venture team) become so involved with the project they begin to discount any evidence that the product will not succeed. In some firms product champions are encouraged to take projects through from initiation to launch. This is a valuable function in that it helps ensure that the new product actually comes into existence rather than being sidelined by the routine tasks of marketing existing products, but again can result in ignoring anything which shows that the product might not be a success.

Product champions are often encouraged by senior management because they prioritise the new product, and keep it near the top of the agenda for the firm, but this system has been criticised by some researchers, who see it as a sign of a failed management who have abdicated their responsibility for keeping the firm up to date (Johne and Snelson, 1990).

There are six broad types of innovation strategy:

1 **Offensive**. Pride in being the first. This is the strategy of firms such as Sony and 3M, who devote large amounts of their budgets to research and development. Offensive strategies also characterise the major pharmaceutical companies, who spend around 12% of their sales revenue on research and development, compared with an average of 1.6% across industry as a whole (Elliott and Beavis, 1994).
2 **Defensive**. 'Me-toos', copies of other companies' products, but with some improvements.

3 **Imitative**. These are almost exact copies of other companies' products. This is a strategy that can only be pursued if the other firm does not have strong intellectual property rights (patents, etc.) on their products.
4 **Dependent**. The dependent strategy means being led by other companies, which may be customers or suppliers, but might also be companies that produce complementary products. For example, Microsoft produces new computer software, so it is dependent on new technology developed by computer chip manufacturers.
5 **Traditional**. This strategy is not really innovative at all; the firm is merely resurrecting old-fashioned designs. Examples might be the Victorian potato-baking ovens which are often seen on the streets of the UK in winter.
6 **Opportunist**. Opportunists are in the business of marketing inventions. They will seek out inventors (or, more likely, are approached by inventors) who have truly novel ideas. The failure rate is extremely high with this type of product, but equally the successful ones can be world-beating and extremely profitable.

Launch decisions are often made as a result of marketing research. If the firm test-markets the product (i.e. launches the product in a small geographical area or a small part of the overall market to see whether it will be successful), this may save money on promotion, but the firm loses the advantage of surprise. On the other hand, if the firm goes for a national launch this means committing resources, and mistakes are much harder to correct afterwards since the brand will already have begun to establish its image. Launching the product in one area at a time is called roll-out: this has the advantages of test-marketing, since the product and/or promotion can be adapted as a result of experience, but usually happens over a fairly short period so requires very close monitoring by management. The promotion policy will be affected by the customer category the firm is aiming for: innovators, early adopters, early majority, late majority or laggards (see *diffusion of innovation*, p. 87).

Whether to go ahead or not with a new product is a decision that revolves around five dimensions (Carbonell-Foulquie et al., 2004). These are as follows:

1 **Strategic fit**. The degree to which the new product fits in with the company's overall marketing strategy.
2 **Technical feasibility**. Whether an effective product can be made economically. Sometimes the product cannot actually be made within a

cost structure that allows the firm to show a profit at the price customers are prepared to pay.

3 **Customer acceptance**. Whether customers like the product.
4 **Market opportunity**. The level of competition the firm might be expected to face, and the current state of the external environment.
5 **Financial performance**. Whether the product will prove sufficiently profitable to be worth launching.

Of these, customer acceptance should be the main criterion throughout the NPD process: if the customers do not want the product, there is absolutely no point in developing it or launching it.

If a product fails, obviously much of the investment is lost. However, failure is itself a somewhat nebulous term – there are varying degrees of failure, as follows:

- **Outright failure, lost money**. The sales revenue from the product does not cover the variable costs and it makes no contribution to fixed costs. This could be because sales are low, or it could be because the price has been miscalculated.
- **Outright failure, major negative market response**. In this case the market rejects the product entirely, and it comes nowhere near to meeting its forecast sales volumes. It is likely to be losing money, or at the least it is not earning as much as it should, and resources would be better spent elsewhere.
- **Partial failure, no contribution to fixed costs and profit**. Here the product has been accepted by the market to the extent that it covers its variable costs, but it fails to meet expectations and does not contribute to overheads or make a profit.
- **Partial failure, does not meet projected objectives**. The product is performing, but not up to forecast levels. The forecast may not have been realistic, of course, and a decision has to be made as to whether resources would be better channelled elsewhere, or whether the product can be salvaged in some way.
- **Partial failure, no longer fits the firm's strategic objectives**. Sometimes a successful product can fail to contribute to corporate strategy, perhaps because the development and launch has taken too long and the company's general direction has shifted. In this case rights in the product might be sold on to a competitor, or it might be repositioned to take account of the new corporate direction.

Naturally, given the risks involved in NPD, most companies would probably rather not have to market new products. Unfortunately, given the competitive environment, no company can afford to continue producing the same products year after year with no changes or adaptation.

See also: product life cycle

REFERENCES

Carbonell-Foulquie, Pilar, Munuera-Aleman, Jose L. and Rodriguez-Escudero, Ana I. (2004) 'Criteria employed for go/no-go decisions when developing successful highly-innovative products', *Industrial Marketing Management*, 33 (4): 307–16.

Crawford, C.M. (1994) *New Products Management*. Homewood, IL: Irwin, 1991.

Elliott, L. and Beavis, S. (1994) 'Feeling frail after 15-year slim down', *Guardian*, 8 November, p. 14.

Johne, A. and Snelson, P. (1990) *Successful Product Development: Management Practices in American and British Firms*. Oxford: Blackwell.

Diffusion of Innovation

> *Diffusion of innovation is the process by which customers and consumers adopt new products.*

New products are regarded as the life blood of any company, and much attention has been paid to the development of these: without new products, companies would only be left with an obsolete range on offer.

As with every other question in marketing, the most important aspect of the problem is the process of adoption of new products by consumers. This is called diffusion of innovation, because it is a gradual process – people do not immediately rush out and buy new products.

Some people like to be first to own something new on the market, whereas others prefer to wait and be sure that the product works well and is really useful before they will buy it. Adopting the product means building it into one's lifestyle, either by including it as a regular purchase or by using it regularly and recommending it to others.

An early model of the adoption process is that described by Rogers (1962). He classified customers as follows:

- **Innovators**: those who like to be first to own the latest products. These consumers predominate at the beginning of the product life cycle (PLC).
- **Early adopters**: those who are open to new ideas, but like to wait a while after initial launch. These consumers predominate during the growth phase of the PLC.
- **Early majority**: those who buy once the product is thoroughly tried and tested. These consumers predominate in the early part of the maturity phase of the PLC.
- **Late majority**: those who are suspicious of new things, and wait until most other people already have one. These consumers predominate in the later part of the maturity phase of the PLC.
- **Laggards**: those who only adopt new products when it becomes absolutely necessary to do so. These consumers predominate in the decline phase of the PLC.

The process of diffusion of innovation is carried out through reference-group influence. Groups and individuals obviously have a strong influence on people's attitudes and behaviour; the history of the theory is not so much one of advancing knowledge about the mechanisms involved, but is rather a history of the way society has changed in the period in which the theories were evolving.

This model is by no means perfect: for one thing, the model says nothing about the characteristics of the individuals in each group, and in fact the groups are divided up on entirely arbitrary lines based on the number of standard deviations each one is from the mean. In other words, innovators are defined as innovators because they buy new products, not because they have any other identifiable characteristics. Second, the research was conducted among farmers, so it actually refers to a business-to-business situation, not a consumer situation: this is bound to have an effect on the degree to which the customer is swayed by the social aspects of being seen to be an innovator.

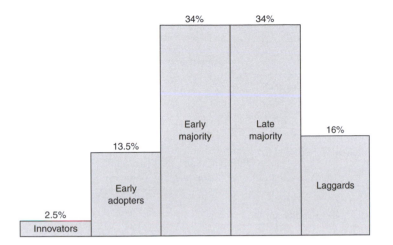

Figure 2.7   *Adopter categories*

There are three main theories which aim to describe the mechanisms for the adoption of new products. The first is the **trickle-down theory** proposed by Veblen in 1899. According to Veblen, wealthy people tend to adopt new products first, since they have easy access to the information needed and also have the spare money to risk on buying something new. In due course, the 'lower classes' adopt the innovation, imitating their 'betters'. This theory may well have held true in the nineteenth century, when class distinctions were strong and mass communication was not well-developed, but the theory has now been largely discredited. Where trickle-down theory still appears to function is in the fashion world, where copies of dresses worn by film stars at premières are copied and appear in chain stores within weeks, or even days.

Trickle-down theory has been replaced by **two-step flow theory** (Lazarsfield et al., 1948) (Figure 2.8). This time it is 'influentials' who control the flow of information. Influentials might include TV presenters, journalists, respected users of the product (such as famous athletes who recommend sports equipment) and so forth. There is, however, a weakening of this mechanism due to the rapid expansion of mass media since the 1940s when the theory was first proposed. In the 1940s there were very few homes with television sets, and commercial radio did not exist in the UK: commercial TV did not start in Britain until 1955, and of course there was no Internet. Also, the two-step flow theory assumes that people are passively waiting for the information, whereas in fact

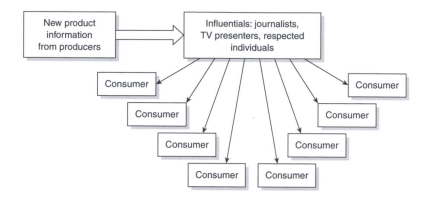

Figure 2.8   *Two-step flow theory*

people often seek out information about new products by asking friends and relatives, searching online, or browsing in stores. The transmission of information about products between people of similar age and education level is called homophilous influence. This type of word of mouth is clearly important in terms of adoption of products, since it is this route which enables innovators to pass on their experiences to early adopters, and so on through the adopter categories.

The **multistage interaction model** (Engel et al., 1995) (Figure 2.9) recognises that some people are more influential than others, but also takes account of the effect of the mass media on both the influential person and the person seeking information.

In Figure 2.9, the large block arrows show the direction of flow of information, while the black line arrows show the direction of the information search. Within this model, there is a continuous dialogue between marketers, information seekers and influentials, with many different stages of information search and supply before the new idea is adopted or rejected. The problem for marketers lies in finding out who the influential people are, since an innovator for one type of product is unlikely to be an innovator for any other product. There is currently no evidence for the existence of 'super-innovators' who are innovative across a broad spectrum of products. Having said that, innovators tend to be more gregarious than most people, and (of course) show more interest in the product area than other people.

Innovators like to communicate about products with other people, for the following reasons:

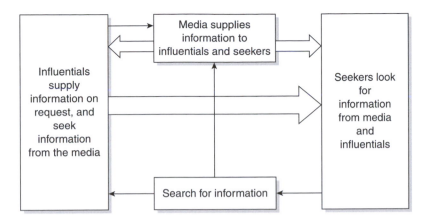

Figure 2.9 *Multistage interaction model*

- **Concern for others**. Innovators tend to want to pass on good ideas and useful products to other people from a genuine desire to help a friend. If there is a close link between the individuals, and the influencer has been very satisfied with the product, this type of help is most likely (Bone, 1992).
- **Self-enhancement**. The pleasure of airing one's knowledge about products is something that helps one's self-esteem, and can earn the esteem of others.
- **Dissonance reduction**. This is about reducing doubts about one's own product purchase. Recommending the product to others helps to confirm one's own decisions.
- **Message intrigue**. If an advertisement is particularly interesting, people like to talk about it to each other.

Actual adoption of a new product is delayed by switching costs (the cost of changing over from the old product to the new one, ignoring purchase price) and innovation cost (the time and effort needed to learn how to use the new product). According to Rogers (1962), people also consider new products against the following criteria:

- **Relative advantage**. This is the degree to which the product performs better than the product it replaces.
- **Compatibility**. This is the degree to which the new product fits in with the individual's lifestyle, values, past experiences and current needs.

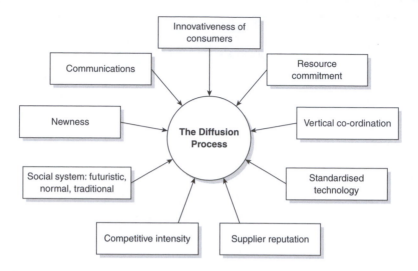

Figure 2.10 *Influences on diffusion*

- **Complexity**. Products and ideas that are easily understood are far more likely to be adopted.
- **Trialability**. This is the degree to which the product can be tried out before buying. If a product is either so cheap that it can be bought, tried and thrown away if necessary, or if it is expensive but can be thoroughly tested before committing to buying, it is more likely to sell.
- **Observability**. The more a product can be seen by others, the more likely it is to be adopted.

Products that score high on these characteristics are likely to succeed: those scoring low are likely to struggle to find a market. There are many other influences on diffusion, as shown in Figure 2.10.

Some of the factors that control the rate of adoption of innovation are under the control of marketers, of course (Robertson and Gatignon, 1985). Competitive intensity, supplier reputation, standardisation of technology between companies (e.g. standardisation of mobile telephone systems), vertical co-ordination of the distribution channel, and resource commitment on the part of the innovating firm will all contribute to the success (or otherwise) of the new product. The speed at which innovation is adopted, and the success of innovation, appear also to be affected by the degree of marketing orientation of the firm.

In the final analysis, and despite the intense academic interest shown in the diffusion of innovation, there is still much to learn. We still have no generally accepted definition of newness, and we still have great difficulty in identifying people who might be innovators.

See also: *involvement, reference groups*

REFERENCES

Bone, Paula F. (1992) 'Determinants of word-of-mouth communications during product consumption', in John F. Sherry and Brian Strenthal (eds), *Advances in Consumer Research 19*. Provo, UT: Association for Consumer Research. pp. 579–83.

Engel, James F., Blackwell, Roger D. and Miniard, Paul W. (1995) *Consumer Behaviour,* 8th edn. Fort Worth, TX: Dryden Press.

Lazarsfield, Paul F., Bertelson, Bernard R. and Gaudet, Hazel (1948) *The People's Choice.* New York, Columbia University Press.

Robertson, Thomas S. and Gatignon, H. (1986) 'Competitive effects on technology diffusion', *Journal of Marketing,* 50 (July): 1–12.

Rogers, Everett M. (1962) *Diffusion of Innovations.* New York: Macmillan.

Veblen, T. (1899) *The Theory of the Leisure Class.* New York: Macmillan.

Quality

> *Quality is the overall relationship between a product's expected performance and its actual performance, as judged by its consumers.*

Quality is the relationship between what customers expect, and what they get. If a customer's expectations of a product are low, then he or she will not be disappointed if the product turns out to perform badly. On the other hand, if a customer has been led to expect a high-quality product and the product performs badly, he or she is likely to respond negatively. Of course, if the product performs even better than expected, the quality will be perceived to be high.

Perception of quality is closely related to perception of value for money. For example, a restaurant meal might cost anything from £5 per person to £200 per person. The person paying £5 clearly does not expect a gourmet feast, and equally the person paying £200 would not expect a basic stomach-filling meal: in each case, though, the individual would recognise that what is provided is value for money. The diners may actually be the same person, on different occasions: grabbing a cheap lunch at the pub for £5 is a different proposition from taking one's wife out for a 25th wedding anniversary celebration, or entertaining an important business client.

Quality is therefore not an absolute. Because each individual is starting with a different set of expectations, quality is a construct between expectation and provision, and since expectation is subjective, quality must also be subjective.

Customers' perceptions of quality will become apparent when they are approached as individuals. Service support is critical to relationship marketing, because it is during the pre-sale and after-sale support that customers are dealt with individually. The front-line staff (salespeople, etc.) who deal directly with customers are able either to adjust the customers' expectations (pre-sale) or correct any problems with the product (after-sale).

In the past, quality was seen as the province of the production department, which led to the product concept (see *evolution of marketing*, p. 10). Under a relationship marketing ethos, quality has become the integrating concept between production orientation and marketing orientation (Gummeson, 1988). Marketing could be seen to be about managing customer expectations: this can be done either by adjusting expectations, or by ensuring that the product matches what the customer expects. Simply adjusting the product is not sufficient.

The intention behind **total quality management** (TQM) is to ensure that the firm and its associates do the right things at the right time in every stage of the value chain. If every stage of the process is carried to the highest standards within the industry, the end result will be a product or service of the appropriate quality. The problem with this theory is that it takes no account of the customer's expectations: it relies on the firm's view of what constitutes a high-quality process. Apart from the fact that this does not accord with customer centrality, it also makes it difficult to make assurances about quality to customers in the company's promotions.

The main contribution total quality management makes is in the reduction of waste, and consequently a reduction in costs, because finished products will not need to be rejected due to component failures. The concept of zero-defect manufacture has led to dramatic cost savings in some industries, but apart from the cost savings has relatively little effect on marketing issues.

Benchmarking is the process of comparing each element of the value chain, including company departments, with the most successful equivalent element in equivalent value chains. In theory, this should result in a value chain that is the best of the best. The value chains chosen are not necessarily those in the same industry: for example, a customer may compare the speed of delivery of a stair carpet with that of a book ordered from an online book store. Telephone call centres are compared with other call centres, not with other firms in the same industry.

In practice, benchmarking is not easy. First, truly accurate data on the functioning of other companies are very difficult to find. Second, critical factors in the competitors' success are difficult to identify even when data are available. Third, at a conceptual level it would seem strange to allow the firm's quality control to be dictated by other companies. Fourth, if benchmarking is adopted by everybody, it will stifle innovation. And finally, the costs incurred in bringing all departments up to the best standards of all other companies are likely to be high, which will inevitably have an effect on prices.

Benchmarking is likely to lead companies back into the fallacious product orientation approach. Consumers do not necessarily want the highest quality at all times – they do want the highest quality they can get for the money they have available to spend, in other words best value for money.

Service quality is often a major competitive differentiator for firms. For example, in the construction industry the specifications for cement are laid down by the laws of chemistry and physics: cement manufacturers have to supply exactly the same product, with very little opportunity to differentiate. The only area in which companies can differentiate themselves is in the service they offer: this may be expressed as more convenient delivery times, in after-sales service, technical support services and so forth.

Christopher et al. (1991) have drawn up a five-stage approach to services benchmarking. This is as follows:

Stage 1: Define the competitive arena, i.e. with whom are we compared by customers, and with whom do we want to be compared?
Stage 2: Identify the key components of customer service as seen by customers themselves.

Stage 3: Establish the relative importance of those service components to customers.

Stage 4: Identify the customer position on the key service components relative to competition.

Stage 5: Analyse the data to see if service performance matches customers' service needs.

Firms need to consider which competitors the consumer compares them with – and these may well be firms in an entirely different industry. E-tailers are likely to be compared with other e-tailers, not with firms selling the same products from bricks and mortar premises: a call centre for a railway is likely to be compared with a call centre for a bank, and so forth.

Quality is very much in the eye of the consumer, and companies need to be aware of this: it is possible to manage expectations to a certain extent, but the real test is actual consumer experience with the product. There is no absolute measure of quality.

See also: *involvement, segmentation, added value, branding*

REFERENCES

Christopher, M., Ballantyne, D. and Payne, A. (1991) *Relationship Marketing.* Oxford: Butterworth–Heinemann.

Gummeson, E. (1988) 'Service quality and product quality combined', *Review of Business,* 9 (3).

Elasticity of Demand

> ***Elasticity of demand is the degree to which demand for a product is affected by another variable, commonly (but not confined to) price.***

The concept of elasticity of demand has been provided by economic theorists. Elasticity is the degree to which demand is affected by another

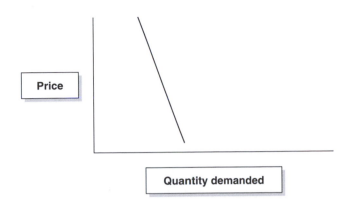

Figure 2.11   *Inelastic demand curve*

variable, in most cases price. It is a measure of the change in demand that occurs as prices rise or fall (or of course as whichever other variable is significant rises or falls).

A product is said to have a price inelastic demand curve if a change in price has little effect on demand. The example most often quoted is that of salt: salt is so infrequently purchased, and is so cheap, that most people would be unaware of a price rise. Equally, if the price fell people would be unlikely to buy more of the product, since the use of salt in cooking is fixed by personal taste not by the cost.

Products that are highly price elastic would show large differences in demand for a relatively small change in price. Usually these are products with close substitutes, and which are purchased frequently enough for people to be aware of the price. Examples might be foods such as potatoes (when prices rise, people switch to pasta or rice) and borrowed money (even a small change in interest rates seems to affect borrowing, especially for large loans such as house mortgages).

Elasticity can relate to other variables such as income or wealth. As an individual's income rises, for example, he or she tends to buy less bread. This is because bread is used as a cheap filler, so as the individual can afford more expensive foods, bread consumption reduces. Likewise, the wealthier someone becomes, the less their demand for borrowed money: even a small increase in wealth would affect this aspect quite dramatically.

In Figure 2.11, it is clear that a large increase in price would be needed to make much impact on demand. Small changes would probably go

Price

Quantity demanded

Figure 2.12   *Elastic demand curve*

entirely unnoticed by consumers. In Figure 2.12, even a small shift in price will make a big difference in demand.

Demand can also be affected by demand for other goods, so elasticity might be measured against demand for related, or competing, products. For example, sales of motor spares will be affected by sales of new cars, although the relationship is likely to be complex – if people are buying new cars and scrapping the old ones, sales of spares are likely to fall since new cars are more reliable than old ones and are less likely to need spares. On the other hand, if the overall number of cars is rising, one might expect the demand for spares to rise, although there may well be a time lag attached to this.

One of the implications of price elasticity is that there is no product with a completely inelastic demand curve. If the curve were inelastic, this would indicate that the product would sell no matter what the price charged: in practice, no such product exists. This in turn implies that there is no such thing as an absolute necessity: if there were, firms could charge anything they wanted for the product and people would have no option but to pay. The distinction between necessities and luxuries is therefore entirely artificial, and (at least in the Western world) marketers do not need to categorise products in this way.

Elasticity is a useful concept for marketers, since it provides a guideline to price setting and in particular price competition. If the demand for a product is inelastic, the marketer will need to compete on factors other than price, since a dramatic price drop (and consequently a dramatic fall in profits) would be needed to make even a small impact on demand. If the demand is elastic, price competition becomes much more

the offer

feasible, but also more likely from competitors. In these circumstances, competitors will usually enter into a tacit agreement not to compete on price, in effect fixing the price and competing on other factors: to do this by actual agreement would be illegal, but to do it by simply never engaging in a price war is common practice.

See also: demand pricing

Demand Pricing

> **Demand pricing is the process of calculating price on the basis of the relative demand for the product, as evidenced by the elasticity of demand characteristics of the product.**

Demand pricing is the most customer-orientated form of pricing since it derives entirely from consumer demand. The marketer begins by assessing what the demand will be for the product at different price levels. This is a job for market researchers, who will find out what customers might expect to pay for the product. Different people have different views on what represents value for money, and will have different perceptions about the price: therefore there will be a spread of responses. This will lead to the development of the kind of chart shown in Table 2.2.

In most cases fewer customers are prepared to buy the product as the price rises, as fewer will still see the product as good value for money. In the example given in Table 2.2, the fall-off is not linear, i.e. the number of units sold falls dramatically once the price goes above £5. This kind of calculation could be used to determine the stages of a skimming policy (see *price skimming*, p. 102), or it could be used to calculate the appropriate launch price of a product.

The next stage in demand pricing is to calculate the costs of producing the product in the above quantities. Economies of scale in production almost always mean that the cost of producing each item falls as more are

Table 2.2 Demand pricing

Price per unit	Number of customers who said they would buy at this price
£3 to £4	30,000
£4 to £5	25,000
£5 to £6	15,000
£6 to £7	5,000

made (i.e. if we make 50,000 units, each unit costs less than would be the case if we made only 1000 units). The costs fall because raw materials are cheaper when bought in bulk, production lines operate more efficiently, more automated systems might be used and so forth. Once we know the costs of production it should be possible to select the price that will enable the firm to meet its strategic objectives, whether these are connected to profits or to market penetration or to some other objective. There is a trade-off between quantity produced and quantity sold: as the firm lowers the selling price, the amount sold increases but the income generated decreases, so the marketing planners need to decide the point at which the price will yield the best trade-off between sales and costs.

The end result is that the product is sold at a price that customers will accept, and that will meet the company's strategic targets. Table 2.3 shows an example of costings to match up with the above figures. The tooling-up cost is the amount it will cost the company to prepare for producing the item: it is the cost of buying in any special equipment or patterns, and the cost of retraining production workers to assemble the item. This will be the same whether 1000 or 30,000 units are made, so it is regarded as a fixed cost.

Table 2.4 shows how much profit could be made at each price level. The price at which the product is sold will depend on the firm's overall objectives; these may not necessarily be to maximise profit on this one product, since the firm may have other products in the range or other long-term objectives that preclude maximising profits at present.

Based on these figures, the most profitable price will be £4.50. Other ways of calculating the price could easily lead to making a lower profit from this product. For instance, the price that would generate the highest profit per unit would be £6.50, but at this price they would sell only 5000 units and make £18,650. The price that would generate the highest sales

Table 2.3 Costings for demand pricing

Number of units	Unit cost (labour and materials)	Tooling-up and fixed costs	Net cost per unit
30,000	£1.20	£4,000	£1.33
25,000	£1.32	£4,000	£1.48
15,000	£1.54	£4,000	£1.81
5,000	£1.97	£4,000	£2.77

Table 2.4 Profitability at different price bands

Number of units sold	Net profit per unit	Total profit for production run	Percentage profit per unit
30,000	£2.17	£65,100	62
25,000	£3.02	£75,500	67
15,000	£3.61	£54,150	66
5,000	£3.73	£18,650	57

would be £3.50, but this would (in effect) lose the firm almost £10,000 in terms of forgone profit.

In the real world the price the market researchers come up with would be the retail price, of course, so the manufacturer would need to discount the wholesalers' and retailers' mark-ups in order to arrive at the factory-gate price. Given that a great deal of actual manufacture is carried out overseas, the company may even have to include shipping and insurance into the price, which would therefore be calculated as a CFI (cost, freight, insurance) price.

Some companies prefer to assess prices on the basis of net contribution rather than profit. Contribution is calculated as the difference between the cost of manufacture and the price for which the product is sold – in other words, it does not take account of overheads. Sometimes a product is worth producing because it makes a significant extra contribution to the firm's profits, without adding to the overheads. Some products carry a low profit margin, and are therefore unable to pay their full share of the overheads. If, however, the product is not diverting attention and resources away from more profitable ventures, there is no reason why it should not continue to add its share to overall profitability.

demand pricing

A further development of demand pricing is the flexible pricing policies adopted by service industries such as airlines, railways, ferry operators and even some hotels. The system works by adjusting the price according to demand, usually by means of a computer intervention. As demand rises, so does the price: if demand falls, the price also falls. The reasoning behind this is that an airline is selling not one product, but a series of products, each different. Each flight is different because of the time and date on which the aircraft flies (apart of course from the route taken). In effect, the airline sells each flight as a separate product, and customers pay what they think the flight is worth. Those who are prepared to accept a less popular or convenient product (flying late in the evening on a weekday, for example) pay a lot less than those who want a Friday flight during the middle of the day. Sophisticated computer systems enable these instant calculations to take place. In some cases flights will be sold well below the cost of production, but since the aircraft is going anyway, the extra cost of filling another seat is negligible.

Demand pricing works by knowing what the customers are prepared to pay, and what they will see as value for money. It tends to be used in situations where profitability, or at least contribution, is seen as the most important factor in deciding whether a product should be launched. In other cases, a product might be marketed because it offers a chance to break into a new market, or because it has a sentimental meaning for the company, or because it represents an opportunity to obtain a return on an investment (perhaps in technology) that would otherwise be wasted.

See also: elasticity of demand, targeting

Price Skimming

> **Price skimming is the process of setting a high price for a product when it is launched, then gradually reducing the price in order to access new market segments.**

One of the most awkward problems in pricing is that different consumers have different views on what constitutes good value for money. Some people would pay a great deal more for a product than the company is asking, others feel it is too expensive and will not become customers: a firm that sets a single price for the product will find itself in effect giving away profit to the first group, who pick up a bargain, and losing sales to the latter group, even if the company could actually drop the price and still show a profit. To help overcome this problem, some firms adopt a skimming policy when launching a new product.

Skimming means selling the product for a high price initially, then reducing the price progressively as sales level off. To be successful, skimming relies on two factors; first, that not all customers in the target segment have the same perception of value for money, and second that the company has a technological lead, patent or protection of its intellectual property which can be maintained for long enough to carry out a skimming policy. If competitors are able to enter the market quickly, the price will have to be dropped too rapidly to enable effective skimming.

Skimming is typical of the electronics industry, among firms with technically advanced products. Initially the firm will charge a high price for the product, and at this point only those who are prepared to pay a premium price for it will buy, usually innovators. Despite the high price, overall profit may still be low because the number of units sold will be low and therefore the unit cost of production will be high. Once the most innovative customers have bought, competitors may be entering the market as they develop their own versions of the product, so the initiating firm can drop the price and 'skim' the next 'layer' of the market. At this point profits might begin to rise, as economies of scale begin to be made. Eventually the price will fall to the point where the firm is only making a marginal profit, at which point only replacement sales or sales to laggards will be made. By this time, competitors have entered the market, and it is time for the innovative firm to launch another product (if it has not done so already).

Figure 2.13 shows how skimming works. At each price level the product shows a standard product life cycle curve: as the curve tops out and begins to fall back, the company lowers the price and the cycle starts again with a new group of consumers. The process continues until either the market is saturated or the company decides that it cannot make any further price reductions.

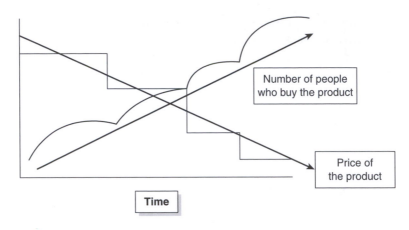

Number of people
who buy the product

Price of
the product

Time

Figure 2.13   *Price skimming*

One of the advantages of skimming is that development costs are returned fairly quickly: in the electronics business these costs tend to be high, but there are also substantial economies of scale on long production runs, so that the product can later be sold near the marginal cost of production. This acts as a barrier to competition, since competitors may have difficulty in recovering their own development costs, especially if they have to find a way of circumventing intellectual property rights. Another advantage is that the initial high price signals high quality to the potential buyer, so that the product seems like a real bargain as the prices fall. Finally, for some firms the initial launch into a small, exclusive market provides many of the advantages of test-marketing – the company can gain experience with the market and the product, and can easily withdraw if the market appears not to want the product (as was the case with the Sony Watchman, a portable TV and video player launched in the late 1980s, which sank without trace).

A classic example of skimming was the Sony Walkman, which cost over £70 when it was first introduced in the early 1980s. At the time, £70 was approximately equal to the UK weekly average wage. Allowing for inflation, the price is now around one-tenth of what it was then, but the product has been almost entirely replaced by iPod technology. This, too, was introduced at an initially high price, but cheap versions of the product are available for extremely low prices, in comparison with the original Walkman.

Recent research shows that customers are aware of skimming in electronics markets, and are delaying purchases of new electronic devices until the prices drop. The price drop is usually fairly rapid, as electronics companies become better at reverse engineering new products (dismantling them to see how they work, then producing their own versions) and patentable breakthroughs are less common. This may affect the way firms view skimming in the future.

Successful skimming requires careful judgement of what is happening in the marketplace, both in terms of observing customer behaviour and of observing competitive response. Market research is therefore basic to the success of a skimming policy, and very careful monitoring of sales to know when to cut the price again.

See also: elasticity of demand, product life cycle

Psychological Pricing

Psychological pricing is the use of an understanding of consumer thought processes in order to determine appropriate prices for products.

The main contribution of psychology in pricing decisions is the role of perception. People tend to perceive a total product, including core benefits, product attributes, support services and indeed the whole package of benefits the product offers: against this, they compare the price. Since many of the attributes of the product remain unknown until after purchase, price is often used as a surrogate for determining quality.

Psychological pricing relies on emotional responses from the consumer rather than on considered calculation. Higher prices are often assumed by consumers to indicate higher quality, so some firms will use prestige pricing, by which the prestigious nature of the product is matched by an equally prestigious price. This is typical of many service industries, because service quality cannot easily be judged until after purchase and therefore the consumer is taking a risk; a service that does meet expectations of quality cannot be exchanged afterwards. Consumers' expectations of high-priced restaurants and hairdressers are clearly higher in terms of the quality of service provision. For this reason, cutting prices in service industries does not necessarily lead to an increase in business, since potential customers may well assume that the lower prices reflect a poorer service.

Odd–even pricing is another example of psychological pricing. It is common for retailers to end prices with an odd number, for example £6.99 or $3.95 rather than £7 or $4. The assumption is that consumers categorise these prices as '£6 and a bit' or '$3 and change' and thus perceive the price as being lower. The effect may also be due to an association with discounted or sale prices; researchers report that '99' endings on prices increase sales by around 8% (Schindler and Kirby, 1997).

Odd–even pricing does not necessarily work in all cultures (Suri and Anderson 2004). In Poland, for example, the effects are negligible. Odd–even pricing also has effects on perceptions of discounts during sales. Rounding the price to (say) £5 from £4.99 leads people to overvalue the size of the discount, which increases the perception of value for money (Gueguen and Legoherel, 2004). Thus the positive effect on sales of using a 99-ending can be negated by the effect when the product is on offer in a sale.

In China, there is evidence to suggest that prices ending in 8 are more effective than prices ending in 4, because 8 is a lucky number and 4 is unlucky (Simmons and Schindler, 2003).

REFERENCES

Gueguen, Nicolas and Legoherel, Patrick (2004) 'Numerical encoding and odd-ending prices: the effect of a contrast in discount perception', *European Journal of Marketing*, 38 (1): 194–208.

Schindler, R.M. and Kirby, P.N. (1997) 'Patterns of right-most digits used in advertised prices: implications for nine-ending effects', *Journal of Consumer Research*, September: 192–201.

Simmons, C. Lee and Schindler, Robert M. (2003) 'Cultural superstitions and the price endings used in Chinese advertising', *Journal of International Marketing*, 11(2): 101–11.

Suri, Rajneesh, Anderson, Rolph E. and Kotlov, Vassili (2004): 'The use of 9-ending prices: contrasting the USA with Poland', *European Journal of Marketing*, 38 (1): 56–72.

Not-for-profit marketing

Not-for-profit marketing is the use of the techniques and concepts of marketing in situations where the aims of the organisation are other than the generation of profit.

Not all marketing activities are carried out for the purposes of showing a profit, although most definitions of marketing seem to mention profit as the main motive. Non-profit organisations such as charities, government departments, political parties and pressure groups use marketing techniques as a way of achieving their overall aims.

For such groups, many aims might be possible. In some cases the organisation seeks to change public opinion in some way, for example a pressure group such as Greenpeace may want to change people's thinking on environmental issues, or a political party may look to change attitudes on specific issues with a view to increasing the vote at the next election. In other cases the organisation might have a specific call to action, perhaps to donate funds or to volunteer to help in some practical way. For example, Voluntary Service Overseas (VSO) sometimes contacts suitable people who might be prepared to volunteer to live and work in another country for a few months or years.

Conceptually, the fact that marketing is almost always considered in terms of financial exchanges does create an element of conflict when considering not-for-profit marketing, but in fact all organisations need money to survive. For a profit-making company, the profits are used to pay shareholders a return on their investment: for a non-profit organisation money is used to further the aims of the organisation. At the end of the year each organisation will have obtained a certain amount of money, and paid out a certain amount of money, and will have achieved some of its objectives for the year (or not). Marketing techniques are part of this process, since business is about people as much as is charitable work or politics: most businesses have many aims – profit is just the means by which they stay in the game.

For the non-profit organisation, however, there are likely to be more stakeholder groups to satisfy. A charity such as the National Society for the Prevention of Cruelty to Children (NSPCC) needs to raise funds from the public, needs to raise awareness of child abuse, needs to lobby government for changes in legislation or practice, needs to establish good working relationships with government and local authority agencies, and needs to change the attitudes and behaviour of parents who abuse their children. These different stakeholder groups may have conflicting expectations, so that pleasing one group may mean alienating another group.

For non-profit organisations, there is likely to be more emphasis on public relations than on advertising or personal selling, and there is usually little scope for sales promotion since there are no sales. In some cases, however, the type of creative thinking that is used for developing an effective sales promotion campaign is useful in developing schemes for charities – for example, a museum may be non-profit but may have a 'Friends of the Museum' organisation, whose members obtain special privileges such as previews of new exhibits, or social events at the museum, in exchange for membership fees and contributions.

Conceptually, not-for-profit marketing appears at first sight to be at odds with most definitions of marketing. On closer inspection, there is little to choose between them – each type of organisation has to obtain funds to keep running, and each organisation has aims that it seeks to achieve. Profit is rarely an end in itself: it is almost always a means to an end, such as growth, market domination, or even simply survival.

See also: *management of exchange, evolution of marketing*

Part 3
Approaching Customers

Need Satisfaction

> *Need satisfaction is the driving force behind consumer behaviour, and the process by which marketing exchanges become successful.*

The marketing concept rests on the idea of satisfying customer needs. In fact, if customers' needs are not satisfied they will cease to be customers – which of course, in the long run, would spell disaster for the business.

In general, customers have generic needs, which marketers seek to satisfy. These are shown in Box 3.1.

Box 3.1 Customer needs

Current product needs   All customers for a given product have needs based on the features and benefits of the product. This also relates to the quantities they are likely to buy, and any problems they might experience with the products

Future needs   Predicting future demand is a key function of market research. Typically, this is carried out by talking to potential and actual customers and making an assessment of likely purchase quantities. Like any other predictions of the future, the results are unlikely to be perfect, but sales forecasting is essential if resources are to be put in place to ensure that upplies are available to meet demand. Equally, over-optimistic forecasts can result in over-supply and consequent problems in getting rid of excess product. Selling off excess product at cut prices generates problems beyond the immediate loss of profit: damage to the reputation of the brand may continue for years afterwards

Desired pricing levels   Customers will naturally want to buy products at the lowest possible prices. Pricing is not straightforward for marketers: it is not simply a matter of adding up what it costs to supply the product, adding on a profit margin and then selling the product. Customers will only pay what they feel is reasonable for the product, basing this on what they perceive to

(Continued)

(Continued)

be the benefits they will get from buying the product. Customers will therefore not pay more than the 'fair' price, and charging them less is simply giving away profit

Information needs   Customers need to know about a product and understand what benefits will accrue from buying it. They also need to know what the drawbacks are of owning the product, but this information is unlikely to be provided by the organisation. For major purchases, customers will seek this information elsewhere. Information needs to be presented in an appropriate place and format, and should be accurate

Product availability   Products need to be in the right place at the right time. This means that suppliers need to recruit the appropriate intermediaries (wholesalers and retailers) and to ensure efficient transport systems to move the products to the point of sale in a way that ensures they arrive in good condition, but at the same time in as economical a manner as possible.

These generic needs apply to all products and all customers: it is obvious from the list that people's needs go far beyond the simple practical aspects of the product and its features. Human need also goes far beyond survival, and in the Western world there are very few of us who have ever had to consider basic survival needs such as food, shelter or clothing. We never get anywhere near to starvation because we eat more than enough simply for pleasure – the pleasure of eating with friends, the enjoyment of the food itself, sometimes the artistic process of creating a gourmet meal are all examples of the pleasures surrounding food. Even in societies that live closer to the edge of survival, needs such as entertainment, social acceptance, the esteem of others and the aesthetic need to create art and music still have considerable importance.

It is the higher-order needs that usually concern marketers. There have been many attempts to classify human needs: Maslow's Hierarchy is probably the best known model. Maslow (1954) classified needs in terms of a hierarchy, with survival needs such as food and shelter at the bottom. Maslow theorised that someone would try to meet these needs first, before progressing to consider security needs, i.e. ensuring the continued satisfaction of the survival needs. Once secure, the individual might seek to satisfy the need to belong to a group, after which he or she might seek the esteem of the group: following on from this, the individual would seek to satisfy aesthetic needs such as art and music before finally seeking self-actualisation. This model appears logical, but in fact needs do not follow a neat hierarchy. We are all familiar with the concept of the artist starving in a garret rather than give up his art, and most of us at some time or other have gone without basic necessities of life in order to meet an aesthetic or self-actualisation need. Homeless people might seek out the company of others rather than look for shelter for the night, and it seems unlikely that sports such as mountaineering or sky-diving would exist at all if people were not prepared to risk their survival in order to self-actualise.

Murray (1938) listed 20 separate need categories. These are as follows: succourance, nurturance, sentience, deference, abasement, defendence, infavoidance, harmavoidance, achievement, counteraction, dominance, aggression, affiliation, autonomy, order, rejection, sex, understanding, exhibition and play. Murray did not carry out empirical research in developing this list: it came from his extensive clinical experience, so much of the evidence for the list is anecdotal.

Virtually all these needs have marketing implications. If a brand owner tells consumers to reject own-label products or competitors' products, the need for rejection is being used. The need for nurturance is emphasised in advertisements for cold cures and soup. The need for sentience is met by newspapers, special interest magazines and TV channels such as National Geographic. Even though Murray's list is long, it is probably not definitive: people have many needs, and it would be difficult or impossible to catalogue all of them. Maslow's needs also have marketing implications, of course: the need to belong has created the fashion industry, club memberships and wearing the team strip. Esteem needs are met by status symbols such as smart cars, exotic holidays and expensive houses: in some cases, esteem is met by a lack of consumption, for example in environmentalist circles or even among backpackers, who may respect someone who has crossed Asia for less money than anyone else. Aesthetic needs are met by art galleries, musical instrument makers and book shops: self-actualisation needs are met by adventure sports, educational courses and 'experience' holidays. In fact, self-actualisation needs might be met in a great many ways, some of which do not really involve marketers at all in any real sense.

Some commentators have divided needs into primary needs, which are concerned with biological functions and survival, and secondary needs, which encompass everything else. Some researchers believe that all needs are biologically determined: if one becomes too hot, one sweats and (eventually) seeks a way of cooling off, whether by plunging into a cool lake or by inventing air conditioning, but some other less obvious needs might be biological. For example, our need for social acceptance probably derives from our former existences as hunter–gatherers, when not being part of a group probably meant being eaten by a predator. Most carnivorous animals display a tendency to explore and investigate their environment, which (for humans) results in the tendency to want to explore foreign countries, canoe up tropical rivers and fire rockets into space.

For marketers, identifying need is the first step in satisfying it. Marketers are sometimes accused of creating need, but in fact this is not possible: needs are created within individuals. What marketers sometimes do is help people to recognise that they have a need. Needs become apparent when there is a gap between the actual state someone finds themselves in and the state they would like to be in. This creates a drive that motivates the individual to seek to satisfy the need. In some cases, people like to allow the drive to build up – working up a thirst makes a drink more enjoyable, and not eating all day before going out for a meal makes the experience more pleasurable. What marketers might seek to do is to remind people that they have a need before the drive state becomes so strong that the individual cannot ignore it.

Marketers also 'create' need when they offer new products for sale. People managed perfectly well without mobile telephones, but few people now would wish to be without one. The same is true of other innovations – CD players, DVD recorders and the Internet are relatively recent examples, but in the past the automobile, the railway train and the aeroplane have all dramatically changed the way people live. No one could have predicted the ways in which these products changed people's lifestyles, but the changes are drastic and permanent nonetheless.

Of course, it has been argued that these products do not create need at all, they simply fill a pre-existing need more effectively than the products they replaced.

See also: involvement, reference groups, product as a bundle of benefits

REFERENCES

Maslow, Abraham (1954) *Motivation and Personality*. New York: Harper and Row.
Murray, Henry A. (1938) *An Exploration in Personality: A Clinical Experimental Study of Fifty Men of College Age*. London: Oxford University Press.

Involvement

> *Involvement is a person's perceived relevance of the object based on the person's inherent needs, values and interests (Zaichowsky et al., 1985).*

In simple terms, involvement is the degree to which the individual has fallen in love with the brand: it has both cognitive and affective elements, since it acts on both the mind and the emotions.

Involvement can be seen as the motivation to process information (Mitchell, 1979), because someone who is heavily involved with a product will tend to want to find out more about it. Someone who is closely attached to a brand will probably tend to seek out (and think about) information about the product much more readily than will someone who is not attached in this way. At a low level of involvement, individuals only engage in simple processing of information: at high levels of involvement, people will link incoming information to their pre-existing knowledge system, in a process called elaboration (Otker, 1990).

The degree to which any individual is involved will lie somewhere on a continuum from complete inertia (someone who makes decisions out of habit, lacking the motivation to consider alternatives) through to high involvement, where people feel very strongly about the brand. At the extreme, we would expect to find people who worship celebrities, or who have a brand tattooed onto their skin (Harley Davidson owners have been known to do this). At this point, the involvement has become almost religious in intensity.

Someone who has no real involvement with the brand or the product category will only make routine purchases, probably of generic products or of whichever brand happens to be easily available or is cheapest. At the other end of the spectrum, someone might be so committed to the brand that he or she appears almost obsessed. This is illustrated in Figure 3.1.

Involvement is not only confined to products. People can become involved in advertising messages, becoming eager to process information and learn more about the content of the advertisement (Batra and Ray, 1983). This would result in the individual acquiring a great deal of

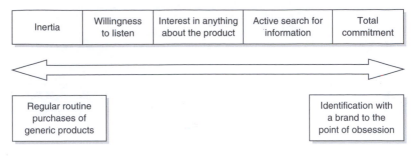

Figure 3.1 *Involvement continuum*

knowledge about the product being advertised. Involvement falls into four broad categories:

1 **Product involvement**. This is a strong attraction to the product itself. The features and benefits of the product are important, for example a mountaineer might be extremely concerned with the strength of a climbing rope.
2 **Purchase situation involvement**. In this case the involvement revolves around the context in which the purchase takes place. Buying a gift for new girlfriend or boyfriend generates high involvement because of the social consequences of making a mistake.
3 **Message response involvement** is about developing an extreme interest in advertising messages. Sometimes this is simply due to a campaign being extremely engaging – teaser campaigns are like this, but the classic example is the long-running 'soap opera' Nestlé used to advertise Gold Blend coffee.
4 **Ego involvement**. Here the product is important in terms of the individual's self-concept. For example, a vegan would be very concerned about the ingredients of various manufactured foods, seeking to avoid animal products.

Levels of involvement are influenced by two factors: personal sources (the means-end knowledge stored in the person's memory) and situational sources (the context in which the purchase and use of the product happens). These contexts can be important: pre-teen girls have been shown to have very specific involvement with snack products, based on what their friends find acceptable (Dibley and Baker, 2001). Equally, most people take great care over how they dress for a first date with someone, and someone participating in a dangerous sport will take great care to buy the right equipment.

High-involvement goods carry the greatest risks since the consequences of making a mistake are so great: this is why people tend to develop very strong brand loyalties. When brand switching is inevitable, perhaps because the brand no longer exists, the individual will need to go through extended decision-making to make a new choice.

Marketers may be able to manipulate some of the factors to increase involvement: explaining the importance of choosing the right pension plan might help the individual realise that some plans may not provide enough income in retirement.

Laurent and Kapferer (1985) developed a five-factor model of the dimensions of involvement. The factors are as follows:

1   The personal interest the individual has in the product category.
2   The risk importance: this is the perceived importance of the potential negative consequences associated with a poor choice of product.
3   The probability of making a poor purchase.
4   The pleasure value of the product category.
5   The sign value of the product category, i.e. how closely it relates to the self.

The authors found that vacuum cleaners score high on the risk dimension since they represent a relatively long-term investment, but low on the pleasure and sign value dimensions. Chocolate, on the other hand, scored high in terms of pleasure but low on sign value and risk value since it is a cheap, short-term purchase. The implication is that different products may be high or low involvement for different reasons.

Involvement can be used to segment markets. Buyers can be categorised according to their loyalty to the brand: brand loyalists always buy the same brand, and would be extremely reluctant to switch. Routine brand buyers usually buy the same brand, but would switch if their own brand were unavailable. Information seekers know a lot about the product category, but no one brand stands out as superior. Brand switchers change brand regularly, having no personal involvement: they simply buy whichever is most convenient, or is cheapest.

It is the brand the individual has the relationship with, of course, not the product. In blind taste tests, most smokers are unable to recognise their usual brand of cigarettes, yet most smokers would be extremely reluctant to switch brands. This means that marketers may not be able to switch people from one brand to another, but it should be possible to increase the involvement of an individual in the following ways (Stewart and Furse, 1984):

- Appeal to hedonic needs. There is evidence that the pleasure of shopping tends to increase involvement with clothing (Michaelidou and Dibb, 2006).
- Use unusual stimuli to attract attention.
- Use celebrity endorsement. Involvement with the celebrity may transfer to the product.
- Use prominent stimuli such as fast action or loud music to capture the viewer's attention.
- Develop an ongoing relationship with existing customers. This is not easy – the history of relationship marketing in business-to-consumer markets is one of patchy success.

Increasing involvement is not easy on a mass-market basis, because involvement is such a personal issue for consumers: falling in love with a brand relies on so many personal factors, most of which will not be accessible to the marketer except in personal selling circumstances where the salesperson is able to establish a personal rapport with the customer.

Involvement can be considered in terms of attachment theory, in particular avoidance and anxiety factors. Avoidance factors are those that make people shun relationships due to a fear of intimacy (in the case of brands, people might become afraid of becoming dependent on the brand in some way) while anxiety factors are those that make people fear loss, anxiety or rejection. People who are low or high on both dimensions report high satisfaction with brands, whereas people who are high on one dimension and low on the other report low satisfaction rates (Thompson and Johnson, 2002). In simple terms, people who avoid relationships with brands, and also fear loss by being involved, will not become involved with brands and will therefore have no problems with involvement. Likewise, people who enjoy having favourite brands, and are not afraid of loss or rejection, will happily enjoy having a lot of favourite brands with which they are deeply involved. There are gender differences in brand relationship formation: when considering the two propositions 'I understand the brand' and 'The brand understands me' women use both dimensions to judge their closeness to the brand, whereas men judge only by their own actions towards the brand (Monga, 2002).

Involvement does not necessarily equate to price. Relatively low-priced items such as beer can generate very strong involvements, sometimes among people who do not care which make of car they drive as long as it gets them from A to B. Equally, someone might spend a large amount of money on a computer system without being in any way a computer enthusiast – it may simply be that the individual needs a sophisticated system in order to work from home, and has no emotional attachment to the equipment provided it does the job.

Involvement is one of the most fascinating aspects of consumer behaviour, especially for marketers: the fact that people become so emotionally attached to the things they own is interesting in itself, but for marketers the possibility of increasing someone's involvement in the brand opens up the possibility of shutting out competitors entirely – a strategic goal greatly to be valued.

See also: *reference groups, need satisfaction*

REFERENCES

Batra, Rajeev and Ray, Michael L. (1983) 'Operationalising involvement as depth and quality of cognitive responses', in Alice Tybout and Richard Bagozzi (eds), *Advances in Consumer Research*. Ann Arbor, MI: Association for Consumer Research. pp. 309–13.

Dibley, Anne and Baker, Susan (2001) 'Uncovering the links between brand choice and personal values among young British and Spanish girls', *Journal of Consumer Behaviour*, 1 (1): 77–93.

Laurent, Gilles and Kapferer, Jean-Noel (1985) 'Measuring consumer involvement profiles', *Journal of Marketing Research*, 22 (Feb): 41–53.

Michaelidou, Nina, and Dibb, Sally (2006) 'Product involvement: an application in clothing', *Journal of Consumer Behaviour*, 5 (Sep–Oct): 442–53.

Mitchell, Andrew (1979) 'Involvement: a potentially important mediator of consumer behaviour', in William L. Wilkie (ed.), *Advances in Consumer Research* 6 (Provo, UT: Association for Consumer Research). pp. 191–6.

Monga, Alokparna Basu (2002) 'Brand as a relationship partner: gender differences in perspectives', *Advances in Consumer Research*, 29 (1): 41.

Otker, Ton (1990) 'The highly involved consumer: a marketing myth?', *Marketing and Research Today*, February, pp. 30–6.

Stewart, David W. and Furse, David H. (1984) 'Analysis of executional factors in advertising performance', *Journal of Advertising Research*, 24: 23–6.

Thompson, Matthew and Johnson, Allison R. (2002) 'Investigating the role of attachment dimensions as predictors of satisfaction in consumer-brand relationships', *Advances in Consumer Behaviour*, 29 (1): 42.

Zaichowsky, Judith L. (1985) 'Measuring the involvement construct in marketing', *Journal of Consumer Research*, 12 (Dec): 341–52.

involvement

Segmentation

> **Segmentation is the process of identifying groups of customers with similar needs, with a view to supplying a single solution to the entire group.**

Segmentation is the process of dividing markets into groups of potential customers with similar needs. The purpose of doing this is to enable the firm to channel its scarce resources towards those who are most likely to benefit from the firm's products. Segmentation is closely linked with targeting, which is the act of choosing which segments to offer a product to.

Segmentation operates at four levels: mass marketing, segmented markets, niche marketing, and micromarketing. **Mass marketing** is almost impossible to achieve in the modern world, simply because the 'one size fits all' products are either already well established, or have no market because people (at least in the West) are able to afford the small extra cost of buying something that is tailored to their needs. The existence of global markets has meant that the benefits of mass production have reduced, since a more customised product can be sold to a worldwide segment.

Segmented markets consist of significant numbers of people with similar needs. Theoretically, each firm in the market will be aiming to satisfy the needs of a slightly different segment, which means that firms should be able to avoid competing directly. In practice, this is again difficult to achieve, since identifying individual members of a segment is often problematic.

Niche marketers focus on small sub-groups within the larger segments and aim to produce very carefully targeted products. In most cases, aiming for a small segment means that the company does not have to compete against very large firms, which tend to go for large segments. Niche marketers are also able to establish close relationships with their customers, and understand their needs very well.

Micromarketers tailor their products to suit specific individuals and circumstances. In effect, this means seeking out a segment of one.

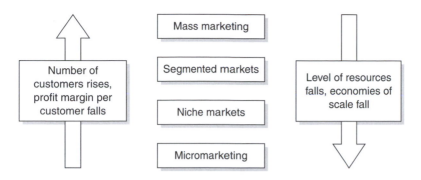

Figure 3.2 *Segmentation trade-offs*

As the product becomes more customised, one would expect that customers would be prepared to pay more for it, so there is a trade-off between the extra cost of providing a more tailored product and the extra price that customers are prepared to pay. If the premium is small and the costs are large, the customisation is unlikely to be worthwhile. This calculation can be a difficult one for marketers to make.

Each level of segmentation has its own advantages and disadvantages, but in general consumers are expecting a much higher standard of service than they previously have, and given the globalisation of world markets consumers have a great deal more choice and variety than they have had before. People (understandably) want to be treated as individuals, and the marketer who ignores this does so at his or her peril.

Segmentation occurs in three stages:

1 Developing an understanding of the needs of customers in the total market. This may come about through formal market research, or it may come about through internal knowledge within the firm (for example from salespeople or others who have regular direct contact with customers).
2 Grouping customers according to their different needs and wants. This is somewhat difficult, since the basis for deciding where to draw the dividing line between groups is not always clear. Understanding the salient characteristics of customers is basic to this process.
3 Groups are selected for targeting. This implies rejecting some groups that look unprofitable or do not fit the company's strategic plans in some other way.

Bases for deciding where to draw the line between groups are numerous, and firms are always looking for new ways to segment markets more meaningfully. The basic methods are as follows:

- **Behaviourally**. Here we are not interested in what the customers think, we are only interested in what they do. If we are selling golf clubs we only need to know that the customer play golf – their political opinions, views on strong drink, or other attitudes are irrelevant. Behavioural segmentation might be on the basis of the benefits the customer seeks, the purchase occasion, or the purchase behaviour. The level of use is also relevant: whether a customer is a heavy user, medium user, light user, ex-user, or non-user is of course useful to know. The degree to which the buyer is ready to buy, and attitude towards the product will also affect behavioural segmentation.
- **Geographic** segmentation is based around the region where the customers live. Some of the factors in geographic segmentation centre around geology: people living in mountainous areas have different needs from those in lowlands, for example. Equally, people in colder climates have different needs from people in the tropics. The main aspect of geographical segmentation of interest to marketers is, however, the fact that people living in different postcode areas are often similar types – in other words, there are posh areas and run-down areas, areas where arty people live, areas where unemployed people live and so forth.
- **Demographic** segmentation is concerned with factors such as age, occupation, life stage, sexual orientation, family size, religion, ethnicity, education and nationality. Segmentation by demography is probably the commonest method of segmenting, but is not necessarily clear-cut: assumptions about older people are notoriously inaccurate, and gender segmentation is misleading in all but a very few cases. Segmentation by income is also widely practised, but again may be misleading since someone with a small income might well have small outgoings and a strong desire to own an expensive car, while someone on a high income might be very careful with money, or might have high outgoings. Religion, ethnicity and nationality have some influence on consumption, but not as much as might be supposed.
- **Psychographic segmentation** divides people according to lifestyle or personality characteristics. Lifestyle segmentation is appealing, because it goes a step further than behavioural segmentation while retaining the same advantages. Many studies have sought to define

segments by lifestyle or personality: yuppies, woopies and similar groups have been targeted in the past. Segmenting by personality can work in some circumstances, for example if an insurance company can identify people who are afraid of burglary and are prepared to pay for an expensive policy this would be a useful segment to target. Again, these groups might be difficult to identify.

Segmenting business markets takes a somewhat different approach, for the following reasons:

- Consumer markets are characterised by customers who are either the end-user of the product or are close to the end-user. Business buyers do not themselves use the product.
- The number of potential customers in consumer markets is usually very large, whereas the number in business markets is likely to be relatively small. In fact in some markets there will be only a handful.
- Psychographic and demographic variables are almost useless in segmenting business markets.

Business market segmentation variables can be divided into two groups: identifiers, which are factors such as industry classification, type of operations, products required and purchasing situation, and response profile, which takes account of post-contact factors such as vendor product attributes, customer variables, application and buying centre characteristics. Identifiers can be ascertained from published material, but response profiles are only available after first contact, and often after first sales.

Whether for business markets or for consumer markets, no single segmentation method is sufficient. Customers have come to expect a much more personalised service than was formerly the case, and firms therefore need to cross-refer segmentation methods to triangulate onto the ideal customer. In business markets, Bonoma and Shapiro (1984) proposed a 'nested' approach, in which the marketer starts with very general, easily obtained information, and moves on to more specific variables which are more difficult to obtain. The nested approach is shown in Figure 3.3.

Global segmentation involves looking for worldwide bases for segmenting markets. As globalisation progresses, global segments are emerging: the global youth market (fuelled by MTV and electronic games consoles) is one example, as is the global executive. In business

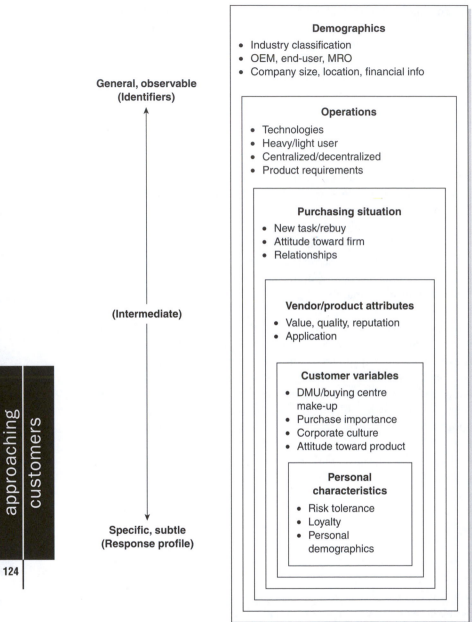

Demographics

- Industry classification
- OEM, end-user, MRO
- Company size, location, financial info

General, observable (Identifiers)

Operations

- Technologies
- Heavy/light user
- Centralized/decentralized
- Product requirements

Purchasing situation

- New task/rebuy
- Attitude toward firm
- Relationships

(Intermediate)

Vendor/product attributes

- Value, quality, reputation
- Application

Customer variables

- DMU/buying centre make-up
- Purchase importance
- Corporate culture
- Attitude toward product

Personal characteristics

- Risk tolerance
- Loyalty
- Personal demographics

Specific, subtle (Response profile)

Figure 3.3   *The nested approach to segmentation*

markets, global segments are easier to recognise because many of the businesses are themselves global in scope, and therefore have global needs for specific components, raw materials, services and so forth. In many cases global customers prefer to buy from global suppliers – it simplifies some of the supply problems and also means that the firm is dealing with a supplier who understands global markets.

The segmentation concept is very simple and obvious to state: the idea of dividing the potential market into groups of people with similar needs and devoting the firm's limited resources to supplying the needs of only a few of the groups makes perfect sense. In segmentation, we are seeking to categorise people according to their needs. The implementation problem here is that it means pigeon-holing people, perhaps putting them in with others with whom they do not easily fit: also, people do not necessarily stay in their segments. They change their needs, change their ideas, change their circumstances and consequently they move out of the pigeon-hole. Other people may move in to take their places, of course, but we therefore need to consider a market segment as a fluid thing, not as something that is always composed of specific individuals. This is a point that often eludes marketers.

The other problem with segmentation is that it means deciding which customers we *don't* want to do business with. In some cases this is because they are just too much trouble, too expensive to deal with, or maybe we just can't meet their needs. Repelling the undesirables is as much of a challenge as attracting the target segment – and again, this is a point that is often overlooked.

Markets need to be re-segmented on a fairly regular basis (especially in consumer markets) because markets are dynamic. New products appear, and these in turn tend to develop new needs. Conditions change, raw materials become scarcer or more abundant, the economy shifts, and in general the world moves on. Marketers therefore need to avoid becoming wedded to their current segmentation bases, and become prepared to re-think the market every few years.

See also: *targeting, need satisfaction*

REFERENCE

Bonoma, T.V. and Shapiro, B.P. (1984) 'Evaluating market segmentation approaches', *Industrial Marketing Management*, 13 (4): 257–68.

Targeting

> *Targeting is the process of choosing which market segments to approach with a product offering.*

Targeting follows on from segmentation, which is the process of dividing the market into groups of people with similar needs. Targeting is the process of deciding which segments should be approached with the firm's marketing mix.

Marketers must decide which segment to target in order to achieve the firm's overall objectives. This may not mean choosing the most profitable segment: a manager may decide to aim for a segment that is currently under-served (or even not very profitable) on the grounds that competitors are less likely to enter the market. There are three basic strategic options open to managers when they are choosing a segment:

1 **Concentrated marketing** (single segment). Also known as niche marketing, this involves targeting a specialised segment of the market. For example, Titleist supply everything a golfer might need, from golf balls and clubs to golf clothing.
2 **Differentiated marketing** (multisegmented) means concentrating on two or more segments, offering a differentiated marketing mix for each. For example, Rocco Forte owns and operates upmarket boutique hotels as well as the Travelodge budget hotels.
3 **Undifferentiated marketing** is about offering a basic product that would be used by almost all age groups and lifestyles. For example, the market for petrol is largely undifferentiated. Examples of undifferentiated products are rare; even the producers of such basic commodities as salt and flour try to differentiate their products in order to meet consumers' needs better.

The choice of strategy rests on the following three factors:

1 The company's resources.
2 The product's features and benefits.
3 The characteristics of the segment(s).

The relationship between these factors and the strategic options is shown in Table 3.1.

Table 3.1   Resourcing and degree of differentiation

	High-differentiation consumers	Low-differentiation consumers
High-resource company		
Mass market	Differentiated	Undifferentiated
Specialist market	Differentiated	Concentrated
Low-resource company		
Mass market	Concentrated	Differentiated (perhaps geographically)
Specialist market	Concentrated	Concentrated

If resources are limited the company will tend to adopt a concentrated (niche) marketing approach. This allows the firm to minimise waste by focusing on a relatively small number of customers. At the same time, the firm is able to provide a much better-tailored service to the customers it does serve.

A higher level of resourcing coupled with a range of segments to approach will lead to a differentiated approach, and a simple one-size-fits-all product will lead to an undifferentiated approach.

Companies with limited resources might be unable to make an impact in mass markets simply because they cannot afford the level of promotional spend necessary. They therefore need to begin with a small segment (perhaps a small geographical segment) and gradually approach other segments as resources become available.

Table 3.2 shows the decision matrix for choosing a segment to target. The marketing mix should be tailored to fit the target market, so each of the seven Ps should address the needs of the segment.

Accurate targeting requires good information about the target segment. Three factors are relevant. First, what are the needs of customers

targeting

127

Table 3.2 Targeting decisions

Segment size	Profit per unit sold	Number of competitors	Strategic decision rationale
Large	Large	Large	A large market with large profits will attract competitors; prices will fall rapidly, and so will profits
Large	Small	Large	This is a mature market. A new entrant would have to have something special to dominate the market: perhaps a much-reduced cost base
Small	Large	Large	A small segment with a high profit per unit and a large number of competitors can be captured entirely by a penetration pricing strategy
Large	Large	Small	If the segment is both large and profitable competitors will certainly enter the market. A skimming policy is best for this market; as competitors enter, it will be possible to reduce prices to compete effectively
Large	Small	Small	This is a mature market, but should be low risk; the lack of competition means that it should be easy to capture a share, and the low profit margin will discourage others from entering
Small	Small	Large	This is a dying market, not really worth entering
Small	Large	Small	This is a niche market. It should be possible to capture all of this market
Small	Small	Small	This segment is not profitable. Unless the firm has something very new to bring to the segment, this is probably not worth targeting

in the target segment? Second, what is already available to them? Third, what can the firm offer that would meet those needs better than what is currently available?

The five basic strategies of market coverage were outlined by Derek F. Abell (1980). They are shown in Box 3.2.

Box 3.2   Market coverage strategies

Product/market concentration   Niche marketing; the company takes over one small part of the market; e.g. Tie Rack, Sock Shop

Product specialisation   Firm produces a full line of a specific product type; e.g. Campbell's Soup

Market specialisation   Firm produces everything that a specific group of consumers needs; e.g. Titleist golf clubs, golf balls, tees, clothing

Selective specialisation   Firm enters selective niches that do not relate closely to each other, but are profitable; e.g. British Telecom sells telephone services to consumers and industry, but also owns satellite time, which it sells to TV broadcasters and others

Full coverage   Firm enters every possible segment of its potential market; e.g. Mitsubishi Industries, which produces everything from musical instruments to supertankers

Choosing the right segment and then targeting it accurately are possibly the most important activities a marketer carries out. Choosing the wrong segment to target, or still worse not attempting to segment the market at all, leads to lost opportunities and wasted effort.

Accessing the target market is another question: for a segment to be viable, it must be feasible to communicate effectively with its members. If there is no way to reach the segment, it cannot become a target market. In some cases the segment is defined by the medium: for example, people who watch *The Simpsons* have a similar sense of humour, and may well be similar in other respects (certainly in their propensity to buy *Simpsons* merchandise). Probably the only way this group of people can be defined is that they enjoy the same TV programme, but fortunately it is possible to advertise to them during the programme. The same is not true of people who enjoy coffee: there is no single medium that can target coffee drinkers.

targeting

See also: segmentation, positioning

REFERENCE

Abell, Derek F. (1980) *Defining the Business: The Starting Point of Strategic Planning.* Englewood Cliffs, NJ: Prentice Hall.

The Marketing Mix

> **The marketing mix is the group of activities undertaken by marketers to create and encourage exchanges with customers and consumers.**

The marketing mix has been credited to McCarthy (1960/1987), but in fact this was only one of several competing marketing mix models that were around at about the same time. Borden (1964) conceptualised marketing as a process of planning, implementation and control but included a total of 12 elements in his marketing mix. Various alternatives were considered and rejected (Frey, 1961; Howard, 1957; Lazer and Kelly, 1962) but finally McCarthy's (1960) model was adopted and remains to this day the accepted wisdom. The basis of the concept is that marketers have various tools at their disposal for encouraging exchanges: these tools can be combined to create an overall 'mix' that targets consumers efficiently and effectively.

The McCarthy model, consisting of the so-called four Ps, is probably the best-known concept in marketing. The Ps are: **Product**, **Price**, **Promotion** and **Place**. This model has been criticised for being far too simplistic: there are many more elements in modern marketing, many of which have appeared since 1960, and in any case even in 1960 the model was over-simplified. The model takes no account of internal marketing, and competition is not mentioned at all: there is nothing about creating and managing long-term relationships with customers.

In 1982, Booms and Bitner added a further three Ps to the model (**People**, **Process** and **Physical evidence**) to explain how services marketing works. This improved the model somewhat, and the expanded 7P model has been widely adopted in its turn. This still does not answer some of the core criticisms of the mix approach.

The seven Ps are as follows:

1   **Product**. This is the bundle of benefits that the seller offers and the customer receives. The particular set of benefits on offer will appeal to a specific group of customers: few, if any, products appeal to everybody. Even products such as Coca-Cola have only a minority share of

their markets, and attempts to create a product that includes all the benefits anyone could want usually result in something which is over-complex and over-priced.

2 **Price.** This is the total cost to the customer of adopting the product. Price is not confined to the cash payment made to the supplier: it also includes costs attached to learning to use the product, to bringing it home, to the peripheral costs (accessories and so forth) and the costs of disposing of its predecessor. Sometimes these switching costs, as they are called, outweigh the purchase price.

3 **Place.** Place is the location where the exchange takes place. Until recently, at least in consumer markets, this has been almost always a retail store. However, place can also mean a mail order catalogue, a telephone call centre or, of course, a website.

4 **Promotion** is the marketing communication package used to make the offer known to potential customers, and persuade them to investigate it further. This is such a large part of marketing that it is often mistaken (by non-marketers) for the whole of marketing. Promotion itself is broken down into a promotional mix, originally comprising four elements (advertising, public relations, sales promotion and personal selling) but in recent years these four elements have become several dozen at least.

5 **People** are crucial to success in marketing, particularly in services, where they usually are the product. Restaurant diners are not simply buying food: they are buying the skill of the chef, the attention of the waiters and even the efforts of the washer-up.

6 **Process** is the set of activities that results in delivery of the product benefits. Again, these are more important in the services environment, but since virtually all products have some level of service attached to them process applies to almost all marketing.

7 **Physical evidence** is the lasting proof that the service has happened. In the case of a physical product, the product itself provides physical evidence, but in the case of a service such as life insurance the situation is less clear, which is why life insurance providers give new customers glossy policy documents.

There is more on all of these elements elsewhere in the book.

The mix is almost always interpreted as being something that is applied to the market in order to win profits, in other words it is something that is done to people rather than something that is done for them. This clearly flies in the face of customer centrality, since it relegates the customer to a role of simply waiting to be presented with a mix of ingredients, rather than taking an active role in the marketing process.

The mix concept has also been criticised by Kent (1986) for favouring structure over process and, as a managerial approach, placing the main responsibility for customer satisfaction on the marketing department rather than dispersing the marketing concept throughout the organisation.

The mix also suffers from the fact that it entirely focuses on consumers, whereas most marketing activities are carried out between businesses (Raffia and Ahmed, 1992). Business-to-business marketing tends to receive less attention because it operates with a low profile: all of us are consumers, relatively few of us are industrial buyers or salespeople. In the B2B environment, success does not come from manipulating marketing mix elements, but from establishing long-term relationships between buyer and seller. If these relationships are strong enough, they act as a barrier to entry for other suppliers (Ford et al., 1986).

Finally, the mix concept suffers from the illusion that the various elements are, in fact, separate entities and that there is no overlap between them. This is clearly not the case. For example, price may at first sight seem to be simply that which is asked in exchange for gaining the benefits of the product on offer. In fact, price is often used as a promotional device (discounts and special offers are often based on reducing prices) and it is also used by consumers as a surrogate for judging quality. In this respect it clearly overlaps into marketing communications, and even branding. Likewise, the boundary between place and promotion becomes blurred when the Internet is considered. Is an interactive website a promotional tool, or is it a retail outlet? Even selling products through one retailer rather than through another provides a message about the product's quality and likely performance. Physical evidence almost always carries a promotional message, slow waiters affect the process element, and so forth. Since everything acts on everything else, it is hard to see how a 'recipe' view of marketing can really apply.

These criticisms do not, however, mean that the mix concept has no value. It does offer a neat way of understanding the overall basis of day-to-day marketing activity, and it certainly simplifies the teaching of marketing. If it is seen as purely a way of describing the day-to-day tactical issues faced by decision-makers in the field, it stands up somewhat better than if it is considered as a strategic approach. Obviously, in common with all models it is a simplification of reality, with consequent loss of exactitude.

See also: product as a bundle of benefits, branding, distribution, demand pricing, communications mix

REFERENCES

Booms, B.H. and Bitner, M.J. (1982) 'Marketing strategies and organisation structures for service firms', in Donnelly, J.H. and George, W.R. (eds), *Marketing of Services*. Chicago, IL: American Marketing Association. pp. 47–52.

Borden, N. (1964) 'The concept of the marketing mix', *Journal of Advertising Research*, June 2–7.

Ford, D.H., Hakansson, H. and Johanson, J. (1986) 'How do companies interact?', *Industrial Marketing and Purchasing*, 1 (1): 26–41.

Frey, A.W. (1961) *Advertising*, 3rd edn. New York: The Ronald Press.

Howard, J.A. (1957) *Marketing Management: Analysis and Planning*. Homewood, IL: Irwin.

Kent, R.A. (1986) 'Faith in the 4Ps: An alternative', *Journal of Marketing Management*, 2 (2): 145–54.

Lazer, W. and Kelly, E.J. (1962) *Managerial Marketing: Perspectives and Viewpoints*. Homewood, IL: Irwin.

McCarthy, E.J. (1987) *Basic Marketing: A Managerial Approach*, 9th edn. Homewood, IL: Irwin.

Raffia, M. and Ahmed, P.K. (1992) *The Marketing Mix Reconsidered. Proceedings of the Marketing Education Group Conference, Salford*. pp. 439–51.

The Elaboration Likelihood Model

> **The elaboration likelihood model seeks to explain the process of attitude formation and change.**

Attitudes are not always formed as the result of a conscious thought process: they can form through emotional means, in other words, a gut feeling can develop. Equally, attitude change comes about from both routes, the conscious (**cognitive**) route or the emotional (**affective**) route. Petty and Caccioppo (1983) defined the cognitive route as the direct route, and the affective route as the peripheral route to attitude change.

The same authors outlined the elaboration likelihood model (Petty et al., 1983). This proposes that, in any situation, the person's level of involvement and ability to process information will be the key factors in determining which route predominates. If involvement is high, and processing ability is also high, the central route will predominate. If involvement is low, and processing ability is low, the peripheral route will predominate. In these circumstances, the individual is likely to be influenced by factors which are incidental (or peripheral) to the attitudinal object.

The model is important to marketers since it explains which is the best approach to take when developing a promotional campaign. If the company is dealing with a highly involved, educated, intelligent audience the best route to take would be the central route. In other words, people in this category would be looking for solid information about the product. For example, a company marketing light aircraft would be dealing with an audience of pilots, who probably know a great deal about aircraft and would certainly be interested in the facts and figures concerning climb rate, fuel consumption, cabin size, cruising speed, reliability of engine and airframe, and so forth. Such a group of potential customers would welcome an informative website, brochures, test flights, and conversation with salespeople about the technicalities of the aircraft, especially since they are likely to be paying a substantial sum of money for the product.

On the other hand, someone buying a bottle of wine to take to a party is unlikely to be as concerned, unless he or she is a wine enthusiast or the person giving the party is knowledgeable about wines. In these circumstances, the person buying the wine is likely to be influenced by such factors as the shape of the bottle, the design of the label, and the price – and very little else, since he or she is unlikely to be drinking the wine in any case.

Cost is not the only issue in involvement, of course: smokers are notoriously difficult to divert from buying their usual brand of cigarettes, whereas house buyers take an estimated twenty minutes to decide on buying a particular house.

See also: *elaboration likelihood model*

REFERENCES

Petty, Richard E. and Cacioppo, John T. (1983) 'Central and peripheral routes to persuasion: application to advertising', in Larry Percy and Arch Woodside (eds), *Advertising and Consumer Psychology*. Lexington, MA: Lexington Books.

Petty, Richard E., Cacioppo, John and Schumann, David (1983) 'Central and peripheral routes to advertising effectiveness', *Journal of Consumer Research*, 10 (Sept): 135–46.

Reference Groups

> *A reference group is two or more people from whom an individual takes social and economic cues for appropriate behaviour.*

A **group** is two or more persons who share a set of norms and whose relationship makes their behaviour interdependent. A **reference group** is 'a person or group of people that significantly influences an individual's behaviour' (Beardon and Etzel, 1982). The reference groups to which people belong provide standards or norms by which they judge their attitudes and behaviour.

Most people prefer to be part of a group, in fact most people are members of several groups. The desire to fit in with the group occurs either through politeness or through a desire to be included in group activities. Particularly when associating with groups of friends, individuals will 'go with the flow' on a great many issues, and usually have similar attitudes and behaviour to the rest of the group. The fear of seeming foolish or of being the odd one out is enough to make the individual go along with the group.

Responses to group pressures may be gender-specific in some circumstances. Fisher and Dube (2003) found that men and women respond differently to emotional advertising depending on whether other people are present. Specifically, men are affected by the presence of others, but women show the same emotional responses to advertisements whether other people are present or not. This is especially true if the emotional response is perceived as gender-specific, for example crying during a sad scene.

Reference groups fall into many possible groupings; the following list is not intended to be exhaustive.

Primary groups are composed of friends, family and close colleagues, i.e. those people we see most often. A primary group involves face-to-face interaction on a regular basis, so it is likely to be a small group: this generates cohesiveness and mutual participation which results in similar beliefs and behaviour within the group. Because people tend to choose their friends because they think in similar ways and have similar interests, primary groups are usually cohesive and long-lasting. The strongest primary group is usually the family, but other primary groups also exert strong pressure to conform.

Secondary groups are composed of people we see occasionally, and with whom we have some shared interest. For example, a sports club or a professional association would constitute a secondary group. These groups are not as influential in shaping attitudes and controlling behaviour as a primary group would be, but do exert influence within the limits of the subject of mutual interest. Members of a camera club might, for example, arrange a trip to an area of outstanding natural beauty. Primary groups will sometimes form within a secondary group; a primary group of special friends with a wider range of shared interests might get together. For example, a cycling enthusiast might have a close friend with whom he cycles regularly: the friends might be members of a cycling club, and arrange with a few other members of the club to go on an evening out. In this example, the friends are a primary group, but met through a secondary group (the cycling club) and formed a new primary group to enjoy a different shared interest (the evening out).

Aspirational groups are the groups the individual wants to join. Because the individual will often adopt the behaviour of the group in the hope of being accepted as a member, aspirational groups can be very powerful in influencing behaviour. The desire to join such groups is usually classed as ambition: sometimes the aspirational group will be better off financially, or will be more powerful. Advertising commonly uses images of aspirational groups, associating images of a product with an aspirational group, thus implying that consumers of the product will move a little closer to being members of the group.

Dissociative groups are those groups with which the individual does not want to be associated. A backpacker may go to considerable trouble not to look like a typical tourist, and a communist may be devastated to be mistaken for a capitalist. Individuals try to avoid dissociative groups, which can have a negative effect on behaviour; the individual avoids certain products or behaviours rather than be taken for somebody from the dissociative group. Like aspirational groups, the definition of a group as dissociative is purely subjective; it varies from one individual to the next.

Formal groups have a known list of members, usually recorded somewhere as a membership list. Professional associations and clubs are typical examples. Usually there are rules for membership, and members' behaviour is constrained while they remain part of the group: the rules and structure of the group are laid down in writing. In general these constraints only apply to members' behaviour regarding the purposes of the group (for example codes of conduct for professionals), and have no impact on what members do as private citizens or when doing things that are unconnected with the group. Membership of such groups may confer special privileges such as job advancement or use of club facilities, and may lead to responsibilities in the furtherance of the group's aims (such as the role of secretary or chairman).

Informal groups are typically based on friendship, and are therefore less structured. A circle of friends only exists for mutual moral support, company and sharing experiences, but there can be even greater pressure to conform than would be the case with a formal group. There is no written set of rules, but informal groups often expect a more rigorous standard of behaviour across a wider range of activities than would a formal group. Being excluded from the group for inappropriate behaviour would, for most people, be a painful sanction.

Automatic groups are those groups to which one belongs by virtue of age, gender, culture or education. These are sometimes also called **category groups**. Although these are groups that have not been joined voluntarily they exert considerable influence on the members' behaviour, because it would appear that people are influenced by group pressure to conform to the group stereotype. For example, when buying clothes older people are sometimes reluctant to look like 'mutton dressed as lamb'.

Virtual membership groups are facilitated through chatrooms on the Internet (Okleshen and Grossbart, 1998). The communication is computer-mediated rather than face-to-face, which means that members can hide their true identities and can (in effect) be whoever they say they are. Such Internet communities can often be more open and uninhibited than would be the case in a real space rather than a virtual space because the social interactions are anonymous (Fischer et al., 1996). This allows people to express views that might be controversial, and of course since the chatrooms are not geographically based people with unusual interests can be in contact more easily than is the case for 'real' groups. The organisers of chatrooms have little influence over satisfaction with virtual communities because this comes from interactions with the members (Langerak et al., 2004). On the positive side, chatrooms allow individuals to discuss issues of common interest, and to share information about whatever topics interest them (however obscure). On the negative side, people can misrepresent themselves on chatrooms, perhaps for social purposes (to appear more interesting or desirable, for example), or perhaps for criminal purposes such as fraud or paedophilia.

There are four types of virtual community, as follows (Muniz and O'Guinn, 2001):

1 **Brand communities**. These are groups who have a shared interest in a specific brand such as a car or computer game. These groups share experiences, offer each other advice and help each other to obtain spare parts, consumable items, accessories and so forth.
2 **Communities of interest**. Typically these are hobby sites: people who share an interest in a sport, or have a professional interest.
3 **Fantasy communities**. These are based on games, whether fantasy games or traditional games such as chess or bridge.
4 **Relationship communities**. These are based on common shared problems and experience, for example support groups for mental illness, crime victims, or action groups who campaign for reform.

The above categories of group are not mutually exclusive. A dissociative group could also be an informal one, a formal group can be a secondary group (and often is) and so forth. For example, one may not wish to become friends with a group of drunken hooligans (who see themselves as an informal group of friends having a good time). Likewise the golf club could be a place of refuge to which one retreats to have a quiet drink with like-minded people, as well as a place where golf is played.

There are several ways in which reference groups affect people. First, groups tend to use a process of socialization to modify members' behaviour. This is a learning process which leads to an understanding of acceptable behaviours within the group. For example, a golf club may have a written set of rules regarding care of the greens, dress codes, behaviour in the clubhouse and so forth, but new members will find out from existing members which rules are essential and which are often ignored. More importantly, the existing members will advise new members on behaviour that is expected but is not in the written rules – for example, buying a round of drinks when one scores a hole in one. Shopping with friends is an important way of learning what is appropriate and what is not: this may be why adolescent females spend a lot of time shopping with friends (Haytko and Baker, 2004). Shopping also provides a shared activity that develops social education, companionship and an understanding of what is safe and what is not in the adult world.

Secondly, interactions within groups help people develop their self-concept. Feedback from others is the basis of our understanding of who we are: how we see ourselves is a result of how others see us. This is particularly apparent when the group has a specific purpose such as a rowing team, in which the members wear team colours and thus identify with the group as well as projecting their own identity. This identity is projected not only to the group but to outside observers. Uniforms offer a way of blending one's personal identity with the culture surrounding the team (Oliver, 1999). Marketers use this aspect of group behaviour to sell uniforms: in the case of (say) football supporters wearing replica team strip it is a feature of celebrity endorsement – by wearing the strip, the individual associates himself or herself with the team.

Thirdly, conformity affects group members. Conformity is a change in beliefs or actions based on group pressures, and it takes two forms: compliance and acceptance. Compliance happens when an individual goes along with the behaviour of the group without really accepting its beliefs. For example, someone who is not a football supporter might accompany a friend to a match and cheer on the friend's team without actually having any long-term interest in the team's fortunes. Acceptance occurs when the individual adapts his or her beliefs to come into line with the group, as well as adapting his or her behaviour. In the case of our football fan's friend, the friend might actually come to support the team in future, having been converted by the experience of going to the match. Acceptance commonly occurs through religious conversions. Conformity can be considered as behaviour one adopts by observing others after joining a new group: provided the advantages of conforming outweigh the costs, the individual will conform. Advantages might include self-esteem, acceptance by an aspirational group, companionship, practical benefits such as potential for earning or saving money, and so forth (Homans, 1961).

Fourthly, people can use groups for social comparison. For example when we consider our wealth or our social standing we compare ourselves with people whom we consider to be our equals in other respects, which typically means other group members. Comparisons may not be made with groups with whom we have personal contact: for example, a lawyer might compare his or her salary with what other lawyers earn, or alternatively might make the comparison with other professionals such as doctors or accountants. The more similar the groups, the greater the confidence the individual has in the comparison (Tesser et al., 1988). People generally value differing views when they are themselves confident in their own ability and opinions (Wheeler et al., 1969), which may explain why some people opt for cosmetic surgery (nose jobs, liposuction, breast implants etc.) whereas other people are apparently quite happy to live with physical 'imperfections'.

Of the above three influences, normative compliance is probably the most powerful. The individual finds that conforming behaviour results in group approval and esteem, whereas non-conforming behaviour results in group disapproval: normative compliance is therefore an example of operant conditioning. Eventually the 'good' behaviour becomes automatic and natural, and it would be difficult to imagine any other way of doing things. Normative compliance with a reference group is what gives rise to the principles of good moral behaviour.

Reference groups will not exert influence over every buying decision. Even in circumstances where group influence does come into play, people are influenced by other variables, such as product characteristics, standards of judgement and conflicting influences from other groups.

See also: *need satisfaction, involvement, segmentation*

REFERENCES

Beardon, William O. and Etzel, Michael J. (1982) 'Reference group influence on product and brand purchase decisions', *Journal of Consumer Research*, 9 (Sept): 184.

Fisher, Robert J. and Dube, Laurette (2003) 'Gender differences in responses to emotional advertising: the effect of the presence of others', *Advances in Consumer Research*, 30 (1): 87–8.

Fischer, E., Bristor, J. and Gainer, B. (1996) 'Creating or escaping community? An exploratory study of Internet consumers' behaviours', *Advances in Consumer Research*, 23 (1): 178–82.

Haytko, Diana L. and Baker, Julie (2004) 'It's all at the mall: exploring adolescent girls' experiences', *Journal of Retailing*, 80 (1): 67.

Langerak, Fred, Verhoef, Peter C. and Verleigh, Peter W.J. (2004) 'Satisfaction and participation in virtual communities', *Advances in Consumer Research*, 31 (1): 56–7.

Muniz, A. and O'Guinn, T. (2004) 'Brand community', *Journal of Consumer Research*, 27 (4): 412–32.

Okleshen, C. and Grossbart, S. (1998) 'Usenet groups, virtual community, and consumer behaviours', *Advances in Consumer Research*, 25 (1): 276–82.

Oliver, Richard L. (1999) 'Whence consumer loyalty?', *Journal of Marketing*, 63, October Special Issue (4): 33–44.

Homans, G.C. (1961) *Social Behaviour: Its Elementary Forms*. New York: Harcourt Brace and World.

Tesser, Abraham, Miller, Murray and Moore, Janet (1988) 'Some affective consequences of social comparison and reflection processes: the pain and pleasure of being close', *Journal of Personality and Social Psychology*, 54 (1): 49–61.

Wheeler, L., Shaver, K.G., Jones, R.A., Goethals, G.R., Cooper, J., Robinson, J.E., Gruder, C.L. and Butzine, K.W. (1969) 'Factors determining the choice of a comparison other', *Journal of Experimental Social Psychology*, 5 (April): 219–32.

Distribution

> *Distribution is the process of delivering the right products, at the right time, in the right place, and in the right condition for consumers to buy them.*

Getting the products to the right place for consumers to be able to buy them is an obviously important part of marketing. Getting products to the right place at the right time and in the right quantity is the function of distribution, and it divides into two parts. First, there is the strategic aspect of distribution: choosing which routes to the consumer will be most appropriate for the product, the brand and the target market. In most cases this will mean getting the product into specific retailers, but it might also mean deciding whether to distribute directly via mail order, door-to-door selling, or the Internet, or whether to find some other route such as brokers, agents or other intermediaries.

Secondly, there is the practical, logistical aspect of distribution, that of actually moving goods from one place to another. This also may have strategic implications, since physical distribution often has an effect on service levels. For example, for many goods (such as steel bars or oil) time is not especially important. It does not greatly matter whether steel takes a few days to arrive or a few weeks, provided it arrives when it is needed. Other products may be a great deal more time-sensitive, for example spare parts for cars need to be delivered to mechanics within hours of being ordered, otherwise the cars cannot be repaired within a reasonable time-frame. Likewise, perishable items such as fruit, medical supplies or airline tickets need to arrive within a short period of being ordered.

Choice of channel will depend in part on market segmentation, as well as on the characteristics of the product. Companies need to supply products to those retailers where their target market shops, but of course the product will only be accepted by the retailer if it fits in with the existing product range and the retailer's own brand image. From the viewpoint of a manufacturer, the retailer's brand image should accord as nearly as possible with the manufacturer's brand: an upmarket brand should not be available from a downmarket retailer.

Intermediaries such as wholesalers and retailers perform a number of useful functions. They break down bulk deliveries into manageable size, they provide their own customers with an assortment of goods, in many cases they carry out promotional functions (retailers frequently advertise manufacturers' goods in their own promotions, for example) and they supply location benefits to their customers, in other words they make the good available at a convenient location for their customers. The net result of using intermediaries is that they reduce the number of transactions across the distribution network as a whole, thus increasing the efficiency of distribution. If it were not that intermediaries make the system work more effectively, they would be by-passed by manufacturers and consumers: cutting out the middle man may sound appealing, but in fact the intermediaries always cover their profit margins by increased efficiency, so by-passing them will increase costs, not reduce them.

Intermediaries may also provide back-up services such as training in using the products (some computer retailers do this), after-sales service, warranties and so forth.

The following factors affect the way distribution affects strategy:

- Distribution adds value to the product by increasing utility (of place or of time).
- The channel is the producer's main link to its ultimate consumers.
- Choice of channel affects the rest of the marketing mix, so it affects overall strategy.
- Building appropriate channels takes time and commitment (especially in a global context) so distribution decisions are difficult and expensive to change.
- The distribution system itself often determines segmentation and targeting decisions. Conflicts may arise between the firm's strategic goals and those of the distributors, especially in global markets where time-scales may differ.
- Intermediaries in foreign countries may weaken the supplier's control over marketing decisions.

In industrial markets intermediaries can be the key factor in the success or failure of the firm. Because twenty-first century industrial markets are typically global, manufacturers have great difficulty in serving markets directly, and therefore rely on intermediaries either in their home country or overseas to handle distribution.

Intermediaries in industrial markets therefore serve the following functions for the end-customers. They:

- **Provide fast delivery**. Local distributors in the target countries hold buffer stocks, so that customers will not be held up by shortages of raw materials, components or spare parts.
- **Provide a segment-based product assortment**. Distributors such as tool distributors carry a wide range of tools for specific end-users.
- **Provide local credit**. Distributors may be able to provide credit facilities in the country in which they operate: due to differing financial control regulations, a foreign company would probably be unable to do this.
- **Provide product information**. Distributors can promote the products using the local language and cultural referents.
- **Assist in buying decisions**. Distributors can often give advice about several manufacturers' products, and can help in decision-making since they are likely to have knowledge of (for example) reliability and availability of spare parts.
- **Anticipate needs**. Because the distributors know the local market, they are often able to guess what customers might need and advise manufacturers accordingly.

End-users in the target market are usually well aware of these potential benefits, and will choose a distributor that is able to meet their needs. This is why choosing the right distributor in an overseas market is crucial for a manufacturer. However, distributors also serve manufacturers in the following ways. They:

- **Buy and hold stocks**. In most cases, distributors actually buy the goods from the manufacturer. This frees up working capital for the manufacturer.
- **Combine manufacturers' outputs**. End-users almost always buy from several manufacturers. This means that they will be exposed to the firm's products even if they currently use a competitors' products.
- **Share credit risk**. Although the manufacturer will offer credit to the distributor, this is less risky than offering credit to the hundreds of customers the distributor deals with, especially since the manufacturer will only have limited access to information about creditworthiness of end-users.

- **Share selling risk**. The distributors have a stake in selling the products, since they have made a commitment by buying the products from the manufacturer. This means that they will be motivated to sell the products, but in the event that sales are disappointing, the loss will be shared between the manufacturer and the distributor.
- **Forecast market needs**. Distributors are close to the market and are better placed than manufacturers to forecast what their customers will need.
- **Provide market information**. Distributors are well-placed to feed back information about the market, about competitive activity and so forth. From a manufacturer's viewpoint, this information is invaluable.

Selecting a distributor is a matter of balancing four groups of factors: market factors, producer factors, product factors and competitor factors. Market factors begin with buyer behaviour: where do customers expect to find the products? The second market factor is the willingness of retailers to stock the product. In recent years retailers have begun to charge manufacturers an up-front fee for shelf space, which indicates the degree of power they have in the market. Distributors may be unwilling to stock the product for a number of reasons. They may feel that the product would cannibalise other products in the range, they may have an exclusive agreement with another supplier, they may feel that the profitability is low, or they may simply believe that their customers would not want to buy the product.

Producer factors include available resources to produce and market the product, and product portfolio size. A lack of resources may mean that the producer selects a distributor who is able to commit resources to marketing the product: this, of course, means that the distributor will expect a much larger share of the profits. A company with a small product portfolio (or a single-product company) may feel unable to establish a salesforce of its own, and may therefore look for a distributor who can handle this aspect of the process.

Product factors might include complexity perishability and special handling needs. A complex product will require a distributor who understands the technicalities of the product and can explain these to potential buyers. Perishable products will require rapid, efficient distribution and, occasionally, specialised equipment such as refrigerated transport: they often also require minimal physical handling. Special handling might include movement of radioactive products or dangerous chemicals, both of which require extremely specialised distributors with appropriate equipment.

Further strategic decisions involve deciding on distribution density. In some cases producers will be looking for as wide a market as can possibly be managed, in other cases they will be looking for an exclusive market. Wide distribution is usually the best approach for mass-market products such as coffee or chocolate bars, since these products have many close substitutes that will be bought if the brand is not available in the store at the time the customer is looking to buy it. Selective distribution means that the company uses a limited number of outlets. This type of distribution works best for shopping products such as jewellery and hi-fi systems, which usually require a specialist retailer who can offer advice about the products, or specialist storage facilities.

Managing the distribution channel means seeking to develop co-operation between the various members of the channel. This will involve:

- Obtaining agreement from members about target markets. This enables members to aim towards a common goal.
- Defining the tasks each member is expected to carry out. This minimises duplication of effort, and also helps avoid conflicting activities (for example using promotions that convey very different messages).

Because channel members almost always have relationships with many other suppliers, co-ordination can be difficult: inevitably there will be conflicts of interest, especially if the channel member also handles a competitor's products. Also, power in the channel is unlikely to be evenly distributed, so a member may well take control or unduly coerce other members. This is not always a bar to a relationship, but it will almost certainly have an effect on the ways firms relate to each other. Attempts to control a distribution channel by force can attract the attention of monopoly regulators, and can of course be challenged in court – courts often take a dim view of the abuse of commercial power, since it restricts freedom of trade and competition.

Good channel management reduces costs, increases profitability and often shuts out competitors. Good choices of channel enable goods to reach customers efficiently and effectively.

See also: channel management, marketing mix

distribution

Channel Management

> *Channel management is the process of influencing and controlling intermediaries in the distribution chain.*

Place is one of the seven Ps of the marketing mix, and is about the location where the exchange happens. There are two elements to getting the place element right: logistics, which is about ensuring that products arrive in the right place at the right time, and channel management, which is about choosing which distribution route is most appropriate, and controlling the process.

Any of the members of a channel can manage it. A manufacturer may have the power to manage the channel if the firm is large and the products have few close substitutes, but in other cases intermediaries such as wholesalers or importers may have the power, because they form the interface between manufacturer and retailer. In many cases, retailers effectively manage the distribution chain because they are closest to the end-consumers.

Because channel members rely on each other, members must co-operate if the goods are to flow freely along the channel. Conflict arises because each link in the channel has its own interests to consider, and short-term advantage might be gained at the expense of other members (although everyone agrees that co-operation is the best way forward for the overall success of the channel). Conflicts often centre around strategic non-compliance (members deliberately obstructing the process in order to gain a competitive advantage), perceptual disagreements (misunderstandings due to differing views on what is happening) and demarcation of decision-making responsibility (turf wars) (Moore et al., 2004). Power and conflict are equally important factors in the management of channels, but are exploited differently by managers (Gadde, 2004).

Channel co-operation can be improved by using either or both of the following methods:

- Channel members can agree on target markets, so that each member can direct effort towards meeting the common goal.
- The tasks that each member will contribute can be defined precisely. This minimises duplication of effort, and also prevents the end-consumer being given conflicting messages.

Table 3.3   Channel power

Economic sources of power	Non-economic sources of power	Other factors
Control of resources. The degree to which the channel member has the power to direct goods, services or money within the channel	Reward power. This is the power to provide benefits to channel members, for example to grant credit	Level of power. The economic or non-economic sources of power are only effective provided the members value them
Size of company. The bigger the firm compared with the other members, the more likely it is to be able to exercise economic power	Expert power. This arises when the channel leader has a special expertise which the other members need	Dependency of other channel members
Referent power. This is the power which emerges when other members seek to copy the leader		Willingness to lead. In some cases, only one firm is prepared to take the responsibility (and carry out the work) of co-ordinating and controlling the channel
Legitimate power. This arises from a legal relationship. This could be contractual, or it could come about because one channel member has a substantial shareholding in another member firm		
Coercive power. This exists when one channel member has the power to punish another channel member, for example by withholding stock		

Table 3.4   Channel management techniques

Technique	Explanation	Legal position
Refusal to deal	One member refuses to do business with one or more other members. For example, a hair products wholesaler might refuse to supply mobile hairdressers on the grounds that this would be unfair to hair salon owners, who represent their main clientele	In most countries suppliers do not have to sell their goods to anyone they do not wish to deal with. However, if the refusal to deal is based on a restriction of trade (for example, if a retailer is blacklisted for refusing to go along with a restrictive agreement) there may be grounds for a lawsuit
Tying contracts	The supplier (sometimes a franchiser) demands that the channel member carries other products as well as the one the channel member wants to stock. If the supplier insists that the channel member carries the full range, this is called full-line forcing. For example, fast-food franchisees are usually required to buy all their supplies from the franchiser, and must carry the full range	In the UK most of these contracts would be illegal. They can be justified if, for example, only the supplier can provide goods of acceptable quality, or if the purchaser is free to carry competing products as well. Some agreements are accepted if the supplier is new to the market, and franchisers can justify the restriction on the basis that it is a way of protecting the brand
Restricted sales territories	Intermediaries are prevented from selling outside the area to which they are assigned. Most intermediaries favour this arrangement, because it limits competition from other intermediaries	These arrangements help weaker distributors, and can intensify competition if other local dealers carry different brands: on the other hand, such agreements are a clear restraint of trade, so may be regarded unfavourably by the courts

If the channel becomes highly integrated, members will share market information and agree on strategic issues. This has been termed co-marketing (Marx, 1995). Co-marketing can work extremely well, provided trust has been created between the channel members, but the following problems may arise:

- Channel members may be members of other channels, which may give rise to conflicts of interest.
- Power in the channel is likely to be divided unequally: domination by one member may have damaging consequences.
- Expectations are sometimes not fulfilled, leading to disappointment and mistrust.

Sources of channel power are shown in Table 3.3 (Bitner, 1992).

A power imbalance clearly has an effect on the ways companies behave towards each other, but is not necessarily a barrier to entering a relationship, nor is it a bar to success for the relationship (Hingley, 2005). Managing the channel in practice can be carried out either by coercion (with the most powerful member laying down the rules and compelling the others to follow), or by co-operation and negotiation. Courts of law may act to prevent attempts to control distribution channels by the use of power as such attempts imply a restriction of trade.

Table 3.4 shows the main channel management techniques.

In some cases, firms seek to control a distribution channel by buying out the other members. This leads to vertical integration of the channel, an extreme example of which is the major oil companies, which carry out all the distribution functions from extraction of crude oil through to sales at petrol pumps.

See also: distribution

REFERENCES

Bitner, M.J. (1992) 'Servicescapes: the impact of physical surroundings on customers and employees', *Journal of Marketing*, April: 57–71.

Gadde, Lars-Erik (2004) 'Activity co-ordination and resource combining in distribution networks – implications for relationship involvement and the relationship atmosphere', *Journal of Marketing Management*, 20 (1): 157–84.

Hingley, Martin K. (2005) 'Power imbalance in UK agri-food supply chains: learning to live with the supermarkets?', *Journal of Marketing Management*, 21 (1/2): 63–88.

Marx, W. (1995) 'The co-marketing revolution', *Industry Week*, 2 October 244 (18): 244–48.

Moore, Christopher M., Birtwistle, Grete and Burt, Steve (2004) 'Channel power, conflict and conflict resolution in international fashion retailing', *European Journal of Marketing*, 38 (7): 749–69.

channel management

Logistics

> *Logistics is the study of physical distribution, and is concerned with creating efficient movement of goods from raw materials through to final consumption.*

Physical distribution is concerned with moving goods in a timely and secure way from producer to consumer, taking all factors into account, including budget. Physical distribution is therefore about organising transportation to move goods via road, rail, sea and air. Logistics, on the other hand, takes a holistic view of the process. A logistics approach considers the entire process of delivering value to customers, starting with raw materials extraction and taking the whole transport problem through all the stages of adding value. The aim is to create a seamless system for moving goods from where they are produced to where they are needed.

For example, cargo containers have replaced the previous system for shipping cargoes, which required a great deal of handling. Goods were loaded onto lorries at the factories, taken to warehouses and unloaded, then loaded manually onto ships using a total of 18 men (eight on the dockside, eight in the cargo hold and two operating the ship's derricks), then the whole sequence had to be repeated at the port of arrival. During the 1970s containers were introduced, which can be filled at the factory, delivered to the ship and loaded by only one or two men. The goods need not be handled again until they reach their destination. This has reduced damage to goods, reduced theft and dramatically reduced costs as fewer dockers are needed and each ship only spends a few hours in port instead of the days formerly needed.

Logistics is central to supply-chain management. Transport and warehousing links are the intermediate links in the supply chain, rather than the main concern as they are in physical distribution orientation. The most dramatic cost reductions can be made in these areas, with consequent improvement in competitive advantage either through increase in profit or reduction in price to the consumers.

Co-ordinating the supply chain requires the following factors to be in place:

1 Transparency of data communication, so that all those involved are kept informed as to what is happening to the goods.
2 A co-ordinating philosophy or set of rules to which each member of the supply chain subscribes.

IT systems enable logistics co-ordinators to track consignments in real time wherever they are in the world. This makes the use of resources much more efficient: aircraft can always fly full, ships can be loaded swiftly and spend more time at sea, warehouses can be smaller because goods stay for shorter periods of time. Another use of IT has been to minimise wasted journeys or part-full journeys: online systems exist for co-ordinating cargoes so that a driver can collect a return cargo rather than driving back empty after making a delivery.

The logistics approach has been adopted widely by global firms. Shipping and trucking companies have redefined themselves as logistics facilitators, which means taking responsibility for the whole process of moving goods from the factory gates to the final destination, using whatever means may be available.

Logistics managers are responsible for some or all of the following interfaces:

- Collaboration with physical distribution. This means selecting appropriate transportation methods, e.g. choosing between road, rail, sea or air.
- Optimisation of the flow of materials within the work centre, in other words organising warehouse operations so that goods move easily from one place to another.
- Planning and organising storage area layouts, and the type of handling equipment involved. This may involve automating the warehouse, bringing in specialist handling equipment and so forth.
- Selection of suppliers for raw materials, and negotiating price levels and specifications.
- Selection of subcontractors to perform specific tasks.
- Organising after-sales activities, including problem resolution with supplied products.
- Verifying that sales forecasts accord with the real needs of the client.
- Developing delivery schedules.
- Developing packaging to meet the need for physical strength and security.

Not all elements of the logistical system are under the control of the logistics managers. Transport delays due to bad weather, new documentation requirements due to changes in legislation, channel members going bankrupt, or even shortages of fuel can disrupt even the best organised systems. This means that even greater care should be taken with those elements that are controllable: these are shown in Box 3.3.

Box 3.3   Controllable elements in a logistics system

Customer service   Customer service is the product of all logistics activities. It relates to the effectiveness of the system in creating time and place utility. The level of customer service provided by the supplier has a direct impact on total cost, market share and profitability

Order processing   This affects costs and customer service levels, because it is the starting point for all logistics activities. The speed and accuracy of order processing clearly affects customer service: this is particularly true in global markets, where errors or delays become multiplied by distance, and by the time it takes to make corrections

Logistics communications   The way in which information is channelled within the distribution system affects the smooth running of the logistics. For example, a good progress-chasing system will allow deliveries to be tracked and therefore customer reassurance will be greater

Transportation   The physical movement of the goods is often the most significant cost area in the logistics process. It involves the most complex decisions concerning carriers and routes, and is therefore often most prone to errors and delays

Warehousing   Storage space serves as the buffer between production and consumption. Efficient warehousing reduces transportation costs by ensuring that (for example) containers are shipped full, and transport systems are fully utilised

Inventory control   This ensures that the correct mix of products is available for customers, and also ensures that stocks are kept at a reasonable level to avoid having too much capital tied up

Packaging   The purpose of packaging is primarily to protect the contents from the environment and vice versa. It also serves as a location for some shipping instructions, e.g. port of destination

Materials handling Picking stock to be included in an order is potentially a time-consuming and therefore expensive activity. Some warehouses have the capacity to automate the system, so that robots select the products and bring them to the point from which they will be shipped

Production planning Utilised in conjunction with logistics planning, production planning ensures that products are available in the right quantities and at the right times

Plant and warehouse location The location of the firm's facilities should be planned so as to minimise delivery times (and therefore minimise customer response times) as well as ensure that the costs of buying or renting space are minimised. This will often result in difficult decisions, since space near customers is likely to be more expensive than space in (for example) remote rural locations

Each element of the logistics system impacts on every other element, as is the case with many other complex problems. If the supplier is unreliable, the customer will need to keep large buffer stocks: worse, if supplies fail the customer may lose production or even customers. Most customers therefore favour reliable suppliers, and will even pay premium prices for this, so good logistics improves competitive advantage either through improved profits or through more loyal customers.

There are two main variables which must be traded off against each other: first, the total distribution cost, which most managers would try to minimise, and second the level of logistical service given to customers. Costs will rise as service improves: there is likely to be a diminishing return for extra expenditure, so there is a point at which further expenditure is unlikely to improve service levels.

Managers balance cost and service level so as to maximise the firm's ability to achieve its strategic objectives. The total-cost approach assumes that any logistical decision impacts on all other logistical problems, so managers need to consider the efficiency of the system as a whole rather than considering individual elements in isolation. The interactions between the elements are described as cost trade-offs, because an increase in one cost may be matched by a decrease in another. Reducing overall costs is the aim of this approach, but there are difficulties.

One complication is that each element of the logistical system is likely to be controlled by a different firm, with its own cost structure and strategic aims. An increase in cost for one element of the system will not necessarily be offset by a reduction in cost elsewhere, since the gainer and the loser are different firms. Even within a single firm, different departments will have their own budgetary constraints – managers may not be prepared to lose out so that someone else in the organisation can gain. Organising the logistical system as a seamless whole will mean that managers immediately run into these problems, which of course places a premium on supply chain integration.

In some cases the business must maintain the highest possible service levels whatever the cost. For example, delivery of urgent medical supplies is not cost-sensitive, but it is highly service-sensitive. At the other extreme, delivery of paper for recycling is unlikely to be service-sensitive, but almost certainly will be cost-sensitive.

Determining the level of service is not easy because calculating the possible revenue gains from an improvement in customer service levels is not a straightforward process. The number of factors involved is large: competitive pressures, customer preferences, industry norms and so forth need to be taken into account. The cost element is much easier to calculate, however, and the net gain can be assessed by combining the elements of service level and cost penalty.

See also: distribution, channel management

The Stages of Development Model of International Market Entry

> **The stages of development model seeks to explain the process by which firms enter foreign markets.**

The means by which firms enter foreign markets, and become truly multinational, have been a subject of study for many years. Because the global marketplace is diverse and dynamic, the study has proved surprisingly difficult: the 'typical' model has been more than somewhat elusive.

Two main schools of thought on the internationalisation of the firm have emerged from the debate. The first is the Uppsala, or stages of development, approach developed by academics at Uppsala University. This model proposes that firms go through a series of stages in becoming international and (eventually) global firms. The stages are as follows:

1 **Exporting**. This means that the firm produces goods in its own country and sells them in one or more foreign markets: it implies the smallest level of commitment to the foreign market. Sales are usually made to a foreign importer, who then handles all the marketing in the foreign country, through intermediaries such as wholesalers and retailers. The exporting firm may not even have been proactive in seeking out an export market: they might have won the business by being approached at an exhibition stand, for example, or one of its own customers (a wholesaler or retailer) might have opened up a branch in the overseas market. The attraction of exporting is that it is cheap and relatively simple for the exporting firm, but the downside is that exporting firms have little or no control over the marketing of the product once it enters the foreign market. Since firms have sometimes only sought out export markets as a way of disposing of surplus product, some overseas buyers do not have a great deal of confidence in exporting firms, since they can leave a market as quickly as they entered it. In some cases buyers are not interested in firms that have not demonstrated some commitment to the market.

2 **Establish a sales office in the foreign market**. Once export sales are established, the exporting firm might become interested in the marketing of its goods in the overseas market. Although there will be an increased financial commitment, the firm gains greater control and will also tend to encourage greater confidence among overseas buyers that the firm is serious about staying in the market, and that supplies of the product will continue.

3 **Overseas distribution**. This involves establishing a warehouse and distribution network in the overseas market. This gives even more control to the supplying company, and also shortens the lines of distribution so that foreign buyers' needs can be met more quickly. Clearly the overall credibility of the supplying company is much greater at this point.

4 **Overseas manufacture**. The company sets up subsidiary factories in the countries in which it does business, to shorten lines of supply and to adapt the product to local market conditions. In some cases the factory will be a 'screwdriver' operation, in which components shipped from the home country are assembled, in other cases components will be sourced locally, to specifications laid down by the home country's designers and engineers.

5 **Global marketing**. If a firm becomes truly global, it sources raw materials and components from the most cost-effective countries, and markets its products to the most appropriate market segments wherever they may be in the world. In some cases the company may identify truly global segments, cutting across borders entirely. The company's shares may be available on stock markets in several countries, and the company may well employ far more foreigners than nationals of its country of origin.

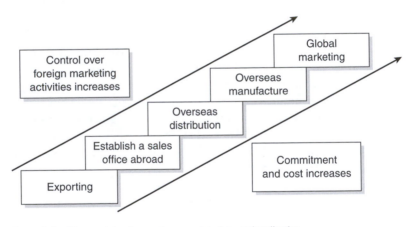

Figure 3.4 *Stages of development approach to internationalisation*

The stages of development theory appears to assume that the company is a manufacturing firm, that it has a strong manufacturing base in its home country and that there are few tariff barriers in place.

An alternative view of internationalisation has been proposed by Dunning (1993). Dunning's **eclectic theory** says that firms enter foreign markets by whatever means are most appropriate to the firm. The decision is based on the firm's competitive advantages, whether in its home markets or in the various overseas markets, and the entry method will be decided without necessarily going through any intermediate stages. For example, a company in the fast-food business might enter each overseas market by setting up franchises, since it would clearly be impossible to begin by exporting. The eclectic paradigm does not assume that the firm is a manufacturer, but the theory also has implications for manufacture since it implies that firm will produce in whichever country is most appropriate or convenient.

Research by Chetty and Campbell-Hunt (2004) indicates that there may be only small differences between firms that are 'born global' and those that take a traditional approach. The differences centre around different attitudes of managers rather than inherent differences in the firms themselves, which tends to support the eclectic theory, since Dunning does not exclude the possibility that a firm might go through various stages in internationalising.

Globalisation occurs when managers concentrate on groups of customers with similar needs, regardless of country of residence. From a marketing viewpoint this is obviously a customer-orientated approach, since country of residence actually says very little about a consumer's needs. The need for mobile telephones is the same whether the customer lives in Sweden or Zambia: only local systems and prices will change. Some cultural elements will, of course, need to be adapted: language and use of the product might be factors that would change as the product moves into different markets.

It seems entirely possible that the stages of development model of internationalisation applied in the past, when the world's wealthiest countries were essentially manufacturers. As time has gone by, however, these countries have entered a post-industrial stage in which manufacture is only a small part of the economy, and services have largely taken over both in terms of employment and in terms of gross domestic product. Even when manufacturing does still take place in these countries it is largely automated, since wage levels are far too high to use manual labour for making things. Since services cannot be marketed via exporting, Dunning's eclectic theory almost certainly applies to most internationalisation initiatives. For manufacturers, the stages of development model is probably still relevant.

See also: targeting, segmentation

REFERENCES

Chetty, C. and Campbell-Hunt, Colin (2004) 'A strategic approach to internationalisation: a traditional vs. a "born-global" approach', *Journal of International Marketing*,
12 (1): 57–81.
Dunning, John H. (1993) *The Globalisation of Business*. London: Routledge.

Market Share

Market share is the proportion of the overall market for a given category
of product, held by a specific organisation.

The concept of market share falls into three sections: overall share of the
market as compared with competitors, share of wallet (i.e. share of the
target consumers' total expenditure) and share of voice (the measure of
a company's advertising expenditure compared with competitors).

For most marketers the key measure tends to be overall market share
compared with competitors. The point of measuring market share is to
see how effective competitive strategies are: if share is increasing, the
strategy is working, whereas if share is falling the competitors are using
more successful approaches. Note that growth in sales does not necessarily mean increasing market share – if the market is growing, sales will
increase even if share of market does not, and in a rapidly growing market a firm can be increasing sales while losing share, as competitors' sales
grow even faster. Growing sales can lull unwary managers into a false
sense of security, imagining that all is well when in fact competitors are
forging ahead.

Share of wallet means the amount of a consumer's total disposable
income that is spent on the firm's products. This is a useful measure as
it shows the degree to which the individual values the company's
brands, and is likely to be a good surrogate measure for involvement.
Someone who spends a large proportion of their disposable income on

a brand is obviously fairly committed to the brand. Share of wallet is a relatively recent concept, and one that is difficult to research effectively since the parameters are hard to set and the data difficult to collect.

Share of voice is an indicator of the degree to which a firm's marketing communication will be effective. It measures the relative expenditure on advertising of each company, providing an overall estimate of the extent to which each firm is likely to get its message through to potential customers. It is a somewhat clumsy measure, because it does not take account of the relative effectiveness of advertising campaigns, but it does provide a guideline for firms in terms of budgeting. For example, if a company aims to capture a 30% share of the market, it needs to plan on gaining at least a 30% share of voice.

Obviously there is an inherent assumption that increasing advertising expenditure will also increase market share, and although this is probably the most likely outcome it is not necessarily the case, since there are too many other factors involved in marketing a product. Not least of these is consumer acceptance of the product – if consumers do not like the product, no amount of advertising will persuade them otherwise. Also, there are many more marketing communications tools that may have an effect on consumers.

Overall, though, market share measures help in assessing the effectiveness of marketing campaigns, and also help in planning, both from a budgeting viewpoint and from the wider strategic viewpoint.

See also: targeting, segmentation

market share

Part 4
Promotion

Branding

Branding is the process of developing a specific set of identifying marks, symbols and perceptions to distinguish one product from competing products in the same market.

The concept of applying a brand to prove ownership of goods goes back thousands of years, but its use in marketing is more recent. The original aim of applying a brand name to a product was to offer the consumers a guarantee of quality, in effect an assurance that the manufacturer was prepared to be identified as the supplier of the product.

DeChernatony and McDonald (1998) offer the following definition of brand:

> A successful brand is an identifiable product, service, person or place, augmented in such a way that the buyer or user perceives relevant, unique added values which match their needs most closely. Furthermore, its success results from being able to sustain those added values.

As the concept of branding has developed, brands have come to mean a great deal more than just a tactical tool to move products off the retailer's shelves: they offer a wide range of benefits to consumers as well as providing a focus for the brand owner's marketing activities. The brand can be considered as a lens through which the marketer focuses communications, new product development, public relations and so forth. The consumer benefits through reassurance about quality, expected performance and price.

In Figure 4.1 the supplier uses the lens to focus the elements of the marketing mix so that the consumer receives an overall message about quality, cost, expected performance and the product's position compared with competing brands. All of this is valuable, in fact essential, information for deciding whether to buy the brand or not. Provided the brand delivers the expected outcomes, the consumer is likely to rebuy at a later date, and also to recommend the product to other people.

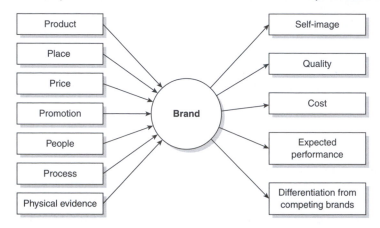

Producer's input to brands

- Product
- Place
- Price
- Promotion
- People
- Process
- Physical evidence

Brand

Consumers' output from brands

- Self-image
- Quality
- Cost
- Expected performance
- Differentiation from competing brands

Figure 4.1 *Brands as a contact point*

The brand can also be seen from the opposite viewpoint: the consumer uses the brand as a lens to focus on the product. This allows the individual to consider the marketer's offering in a critical and complete manner.

In many cases core products have little to differentiate them from competing products. For example, petrol is much the same whether it is supplied by BP, Shell, Elf, Repsol or Statoil: the differences cannot be apparent simply because all cars have to be able to run on any of the fuels. The sole differentiator therefore is the corporate brand, and to some extent the service aspects (petrol station shops etc.) which surround the basic product. The brand does add real value to the product, of course: in some cases the brand carries an image that transfers in part to the purchaser, for example prestigious brands such as Nike or Porsche convey an upmarket image which is immediately identifiable and which marks out the purchaser as a discerning individual. In some cases this is the only benefit the brand has over its rivals, since the actual performance of the product is indistinguishable from its competitors.

Brands can be looked at in a number of different ways. Box 4.1 shows eight different strategic functions of brands.

Box 4.1 Strategic functions of brands

Brand as a sign of ownership Brands began as a sign of ownership, but developed into a way of showing who had responsibility for the quality of the product. This was also a way of protecting the product from counterfeiting in cases where intellectual property protection was insufficient. In recent years brands also let customers know whether they are buying a manufacturer's brand or a retailer's own brand

Brand as a differentiating device   A strong brand undoubtedly does differentiate the product from similar products, but having a strong brand name is not enough. The product itself also needs to be different in some way; the brand image is the communicating device that conveys the difference to the consumer

Brand as a functional device   Branding can be used to communicate functional capability. In other words, the brand conveys an image of its quality and expected performance to the consumer

Brand as a symbolic device   Some brands are used to convey a particular image of the consumer. This is particularly apparent in the 'designer' clothes industry – an ordinary pair of jeans acquires added value because the name of the designer is printed on them. Consumers who believe that the brand's value lies in its communication ability spend considerable time and effort in choosing the brand with the right image

Brand as a risk reducer   Buying a strongly branded product offers the consumer a degree of reassurance about both the product and the producer. Although any purchase carries an element of risk, branded goods do have the advantage that the manufacturer is readily identified: skilled marketers will address the risks that are most relevant to the target group of consumers

Brand as a shorthand device   Brands are used as a way of 'tagging' information about a product in the consumers' memories. This is particularly relevant when the brand is extended to other product categories, since the consumer's view of the parent brand is transferred to the new brand

Brand as a legal device   Brands give a certain amount of legal protection to the producer even when the formulation of the product cannot. Strong branding therefore offers some protection for the firm's intellectual property

Brand as a strategic device   The assets constituting the brand can be identified and managed so that the brand maintains and builds on the added value which it represents

Branding clearly has advantages for the manufacturer and the retailer, since it helps to differentiate the product from competitors' products. Economies of scale and scope are attributed to branding, and a brand with high sales will generate production economies (Demsetz, 1973). A successful brand creates a barrier to entry, so that competitors find it harder to enter the market (Demsetz, 1982): since a strong brand means that the firm does not have to compete solely on price, profit margins are likely to remain higher (Mercer, 1992).

Furthermore, brands that are held in high esteem tend to be more consistent in their sales, riding over the ups and downs of the market place (Png and Reitman, 1995). Not all brands are priced at a premium, of course; many brands are competitively priced in order to take advantage of consistent sales.

For the consumer, branding means that it is easy to recognise the product, and easy to identify with it. Messages about the formulation and benefits are clearly conveyed, and in most cases the use of a particular brand says something about the consumer (Bagwell and Bernheim, 1996). Because most purchases only involve limited problem-solving behaviour, branding helps to reduce the decision-making time and also the effort of evaluating competing products. Consumers who either do not want to spend time on an extended information search, or who do not have the expertise to do so, can use the brand as an implicit guarantee of quality (Png and Reitman, 1995).

That branding works is not in doubt. Owners of a well-established brand can command premium prices, and typically enjoy higher sales and greater security of sales than unbranded (or commodity) goods. Figure 4.2 illustrates the reasons for this.

Branded products have both higher price differentiation and higher product and image differentiation than do commodity goods. Obviously there is a catch in the sense that establishing a brand is far from being a cheap exercise – there is usually substantial expenditure on promotion and product development.

From a strategic viewpoint, the brand image provides a focus for the creative energies of the marketing team. The difficulty for marketers is that product and brand development is often a team process, and as such the team needs to keep a firm picture of what the product is intended to convey – the 'personality' of the product – if they are to maintain consistency in the creative activities.

Semiotics (the study of signs and their values) is useful in understanding how branding works. There are four signs of brands in terms of semiotics:

1   **A utilitarian sign**. Utilitarian signs are about the practical aspects of the product, i.e. its performance, its quality, its reliability and so forth.

2 **A commercial sign.** Commercial signs are concerned with the exchange value of the product (its price, its value in use, value for money and so forth).

3 **A socio-cultural sign.** This is about the social effects of owning and using the brand.

4 **A mythical sign.** Myths are the stories that grow up around a brand, providing a conceptual framework through which the contradictions of life can be resolved.

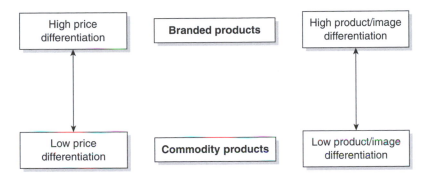

Figure 4.2 *Commodity products* vs. *branded products*

Brand planning is important, but time-consuming; often the job is given to brand managers, many of whom are young and inexperienced. Developing the brand is a process of integrating a number of strands of business activity, so a clear idea of the brand image is essential, as is a long-term view. To see branding as merely being about design or advertising or naming is inadequate and short-sighted; successful brands are those that allow the consumer to focus on the corporation and the product. Constant evaluation of the image seen through the lens is essential if the brand is to retain its status.

Branding has sometimes been criticised by non-marketers because it can be seen to be manipulative, adding costs to a basic product without actually adding any concrete benefits. It is certainly true that the value added by branding is psychological: the reassurance that the product is of suitable quality and performance, and the intangible social benefits that accrue from being seen to use a good brand, are not things that can readily be calculated. They are nonetheless real.

See also: communications mix

branding

167

REFERENCES

Bagwell, L.S. and Bernheim, B.D. (1996) 'Veblen effects in a theory of conspicuous consumption', *American Economic Review*, 86: 349–73.

DeChernatony, L. and McDonald, M. (1998) *Creating Powerful Brands*, 2nd edn Oxford: Butterworth–Heinemann.

Demsetz, H. (1973) 'Industry structure, market rivalry and public policy', *Journal of Law and Economics*, 16 (1): 1–9.

Demsetz, H. (1982) 'Barriers to entry', *American Economic Review*, 72: 47–57.

Mercer, D. (1992) *Marketing Management*. Oxford: Blackwell.

Png, J.P. and Reitman, D. (1995) 'Why are some products branded and others not?', *Journal of Law and Economics*, 38: 207–24.

Brand Personality

> **Brand personality is a combination of all the perceptions and beliefs that customers have about the brand.**

Brand personality goes beyond brand image, however: brand personality implies that people can think of a brand in the same way as they might think of a person. Aaker (1997) defined brand personality as 'the set of human characteristics associated with a brand'. The ability of a brand to make a meaningful connection with customers is based on its character, not on its outward appearance: a brand can have a catchy name and good packaging, but still not have a basic personality that appeals to customers.

Brand personality acts as a form of self-expression. If someone uses a brand conspicuously, he or she is (in effect) associating his or her own personality with that of the brand, in the same way that people express their own personalities by associating with people of a similar type. The brand personality also acts as a reassurance: the imagery surrounding the brand reassures customers that the brand is socially acceptable. For example, the Ford brand has a personality that centres around reliable, no-frills engineering for comfortable, safe family cars.

Brand personality also serves to communicate functional aspects of the brand. A brand that appears to be gentle, environmentally friendly and natural appeals to people with similar personalities because they feel confident in the functioning of the brand.

The personality of the brand is what drives the relationship with the customer. People can, and do, have relationships with brands in the same way as they have relationships with each other, and the brand personality is as important in forming and strengthening these relationships as is the personality of one's friends.

Television advertising is particularly useful for conveying brand personality, because it is a good medium for encouraging emotional responses. The brand personality can be developed by association with its users (showing a particular type of person using the brand, for example) or directly, by giving the brand a persona. This can be done by providing the product with a human face (for example, Mr. Muscle cleaning products have an actual person on the product), or by providing the product with a cartoon type persona of its own such as the Mr. Peanut character used on Planter's Nuts.

There has been considerable academic interest in the concept of brand personality. Beldona and Wysong (2007) found that brand personality was stronger for national brands than for store brands, and Aaker (1997) identified the five main dimensions of brand personality (sincerity, excitement, competence, ruggedness and sophistication). While brand personality undoubtedly has other dimensions, these were found to be the 'big five' in terms of consumer perceptions.

Brand personality is an important concept for practitioners because it can act as a co-ordinating factor for everyone concerned with the brand. For example, when Honda was developing the Civic, the firm had to co-ordinate the activities of hundreds of designers, engineers and marketers. Honda used the brand personality 'Rugby player in a dinner suit' to convey an image of sophisticated ruggedness in a clear and accessible manner. Advertising creatives would almost always expect the brand personality to be made clear to them as part of the brief, and PR officers would also find it useful when planning sponsorship associations or joint ventures. Of course, it is not always the company that develops the brand personality: sometimes (in fact often) a brand personality is developed more by consumers and the general public than by the company, and in many cases this brand personality may not be one the company would have chosen.

See also: branding, elaboration likelihood model

REFERENCES

Aaker, J. L. (1997) 'Dimensions of brand personality', *Journal of Marketing Research*, 34 (3): 347–56.

Beldona, Sri and Wysong, Scott (2007) 'Putting the 'brand' back into store brands: an exploratory examination of store brands and brand personality', *Journal of Product and Brand Management*, 16 (4/5): 226–35.

Positioning

> **Positioning is the process of establishing a brand in the minds of its consumers in an appropriate relationship to competing brands.**

The positioning of a product in customers' minds is key to its success or failure in the market. Position is the place the product occupies relative to its competitors, and it is only in terms of consumer perception that position has any meaning. Positioning means putting the product into the appropriate position in the consumer's mind.

Positioning means that the firm needs to develop a theme that will provide a 'meaningful distinction for customers' (Day, 1990). Ries and Trout (2001) stated that many products already have a distinctive position in the mind of the customer, and that these positions are often difficult to dislodge.

According to Blankson and Kalafatis (2004), there are eight generic factors that are used in positioning products, as follows

1 Top of the range.
2 Service.
3 Value for money.
4 Reliability.
5 Attractiveness.

6   Country of origin.
7   Brand name.
8   Selectivity.

These elements in a positioning strategy are not mutually exclusive, but obviously a firm is unlikely to be able to use all the factors, partly because no brand would be able to position on all the dimensions, and partly because such a claim would lack credibility. For example, claiming to be top of the range and still offer best value for money might seem unlikely to the average consumer.

Ries and Trout go on to say that competitors have three possible strategies they may follow:

1   Strengthen the current leadership place by reinforcing the original concepts that led to consumers locating the brand in the lead position.
2   Establish a new position – *'cherchez les creneaux'* – look for new 'crannies' in a market, or positions that are currently unoccupied.
3   De-position or re-position the competition. This can be done by careful comparison advertising, or by suitable press releases.

Ries and Trout claim that customers establish a ladder for each product category on which they establish possible suppliers as first, second or third level. This can offer an opportunity for positioning, the most famous example of which is provided by car hire company, Avis. When Avis entered the market Hertz was positioned as the leading car rental firm. Although Avis was one of many other competitors, they chose to position themselves as 'number two', using the strap line: 'We're Number Two, so we try harder'. Avis quickly established itself as the first alternative to Hertz in the minds of customers. This is also known as establishing the 'against' position – Avis placing themselves directly against Hertz.

Value disciplines are the elements by which position is created (Treacy and Wiersema, 1993). There are three value disciplines, according to these authors: operational excellence (which means efficient operations, service and customer support), customer intimacy (the degree to which the firm understands customer need) or product leadership (the quality of benefits offered by the product itself). They recommend that a firm should try to become a 'champion' in one of these areas while simply meeting industry standards in the other two.

A perceptual map is the picture an individual has in mind about the structure of the world. Each item in the individual's mind is

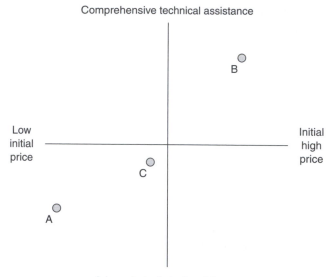

Comprehensive technical assistance

Low
initial
price

Initial
high
price

B

C

A

Adequate technical assistance

Figure 4.3   *Perceptual map*

mapped against other items, creating an overall view of how things relate. Product positioning is based upon a series of perceptual maps. An example is shown in Figure 4.3. This example shows two important variables: the horizontal axis for initial price and the vertical axis for technical assistance. It is obvious that the lower right hand corner of this matrix is probably a poor position to be in. In this quadrant, a firm would be offering a high initial price with only adequate technical assistance. In this example, there are three firms in the market.

Firm A is a low-priced firm offering little technical assistance. Firm B is a higher-priced firm with very good technical assistance. The management of Firm C may see an opportunity to stake out a position as a somewhat lower price offering than B with somewhat better technical assistance than A. Obviously a firm that could offer a low price and comprehensive technical assistance would be in a very strong position, but since this technical assistance is an expensive proposition it is unlikely that such a firm would be viable.

Of course, customers must place value on the variables being examined. If an individual customer does not value technical assistance (perhaps because he or she is sufficiently skilled to be able to handle technical problems unaided) the belief that one firm offers technical assistance and the other does not would be irrelevant. However, if Firm C's market research shows that technical assistance and initial price are critical variables in the decision-making process, correct positioning on this map is important in developing a position that can be clearly communicated to potential customers.

Positioning a brand relies on four factors (the four Cs of positioning):

1 **Clarity**. It must be obvious to the consumers (or customers) what the brand is and where it sits relative to other brands.
2 **Credibility**. The position must be logical and believable – an obviously cheap and basic product cannot position itself as a premium brand. The reverse is also true – few people would believe that a well-designed and well-made product can be sold for a low price: most people would suspect a catch!
3 **Consistency**. Whatever position is adopted, the marketers must maintain a consistent brand message.
4 **Competitiveness**. Successful positioning should mean that the company is not trying to occupy a position already taken by a competitor – it is far better to find a position that is currently not subject to competition.

Provided the company has a brand message that is clear, consistent, credible and competitive the positioning will be successful and the brand will sell.

See also: segmentation, targeting, competitive advantage

REFERENCES

Blankson, Charles and Kalafatis, Stavros P. (2004) 'The development and validation of a scale measuring consumer/customer derived generic typology of positioning strategies', *Journal of Marketing Management*, 20 (1): 5–43.
Day, George S. (1990) *Market-Driven Strategy: Process for Creating Value*. New York: Free Press.
Ries, Al and Trout, Jack (2001) *Positioning: The Battle for Your Mind*. New York: McGraw–Hill.
Treacy, Michael and Wiersema, Fred (1993) 'Customer Intimacy and Other Value Disciplines,' *Harvard Business Review*, 71 (1): 84–93.

positioning

The Communications Mix

The communications mix is the combination of those elements of marketing activities concerned with sending and receiving messages from customers and other stakeholders.

The communications mix is a subdivision of the marketing mix. The basic mix consists of advertising, sales promotion, personal selling and public relations: this list was first compiled in the late 1960s and has been added to (and also widely criticised) ever since.

The basic concept assumes that, like the marketing mix, the communications mix represents a combination of tactical tools which are available to marketers for the purpose of marketing communications. The theory is that marketers can combine the various elements to obtain maximum impact, particularly by creating an integrated campaign in which the same message is offered by several different routes. The intention here is not only to create redundancy (ensuring that a message gets through by sending it through several different routes) but also to enable the marketers to send different parts of the message by different routes, as appropriate. Integrated marketing communications also helps ensure that the recipients do not become confused by receiving several different messages from the same source. This thrust towards integrated marketing communications has been the subject of considerable interest from marketing academics in recent years.

The communication mix model suffers from a number of weaknesses. First, as with the marketing mix, there is considerable doubt that the various elements are actually discrete. There is considerable overlap between public relations and advertising, for example, and between advertising and sales promotion. Second, the four-item list is by no means comprehensive. When it was first compiled, in 1968, there was no Internet, slogans on T-shirts were almost unknown, telephone selling was in its infancy, ambient advertising was unknown, and commercial television was limited to one channel in the UK.

promotion

174

A more comprehensive taxonomy of communication is shown in Box 4.2.

Box 4.2   Elements of the communications mix

Advertising   A paid insertion of a message in a medium

Ambient advertising   Messages placed on items such as bus tickets, stamp franking, till receipts, petrol pump nozzles and so forth. Any message that forms part of the environment – for example, 'art installations' in city centres

Press advertising   Any paid message that appears in a newspaper or magazine

TV advertising   Commercial messages shown in the breaks during and between TV programmes

Radio advertising   Sound-only advertisements broadcast on radio

Outdoor advertising   Billboards, bus shelters, flyposters etc.

Transport advertising   Posters in stations and inside buses and trains.

Outside transport advertising   Posters on buses and taxis, and in some countries the sides of trains

Press releases   News stories about a firm or its products

Public relations   The planned and sustained effort to establish and maintain goodwill and mutual understanding between an organisation and its publics (Institute of Public Relations, 1984)

Sponsorship   Funding of arts events, sporting events etc. in exchange for publicity and prestige

Sales promotions   Activities designed to give a temporary boost to sales, such as money-off coupons, free samples, two-for-the-price-of-one promotions etc.

Personal selling   Face-to-face communications between buyers and sellers designed to ascertain and meet customers' needs on a one-to-one basis

Key account management   Establishing long-term relationships with customers who have added importance due to their monetary value or strategic importance

(Continued)

Database marketing Profiling customers onto a database and sending out personalised mailings or other communications to them

Telemarketing Inbound (helpline, telephone ordering) or outbound (tele-canvassing, teleselling) telephone calls

e-commerce Use of websites to promote and/or sell products

Off-the-screen selling Using TV adverts linked to inbound telephone operations to sell goods. Also home shopping channels such as QVC

Exhibitions and trade fairs Companies take stands at trade fairs to display new products, meet consumers and customers, and raise the company profle with interested parties

Corporate identity The overall image that the company projects; the company's 'personality'

Branding The mechanism by which marketing communications are co-ordinated

A second criticism is that some elements may not belong in the communication mix at all. Personal selling, for example, has moved on considerably since 1968. At that time the purpose of selling was to persuade people to buy products, using an engaging and persuasive sales pitch followed by a series of slick closing techniques. In this model, the salesperson's role is almost entirely concerned with tailoring an existing message to fit the customer's circumstances, prejudices and information needs. In recent years this approach has been replaced by a problem-solving approach, in which the salesperson seeks to identify customer need and supply a solution, chosen from the company's range of products if possible. Salespeople thus do not have a communications role as such (although communication is obviously a large part of what they do) but rather they have a problem-solving role.

A final criticism of the communications mix concept is that it fails to take account of the true nature of communication. It assumes that communication is something that is done to consumers, rather than something that is a co-creation of reality, between the consumers and the company. This is inconsistent with customer centrality.

The communications mix can, however, be a useful concept in that it illustrates the day-to-day reality of communications planning. Marketers are not faced with a choice of either using one tactical tool or using another: in most cases, the communications problem requires a more eclectic approach, using several different methods to communicate a single message. Either the message will be sent by different routes in order to generate redundancy, or separate parts of the message will be sent by the various routes in order to create an integrated whole. If an integrated marketing approach is followed, the messages will reinforce each other and create a more powerful overall impression than would otherwise be the case: this is the ideal situation from the viewpoint of the marketers. In practice, this is somewhat difficult to achieve, not least because the medium becomes part of the message, in other words the message itself is affected by the medium used.

For example, an advertisement shown on TV will convey a different message from the same advertisement shown in a cinema. The ambience is different, the occasion is different (a night out being different in nature from a night in) and the audience cannot zap the advertisement, change channels or leave the room very easily if they are in a cinema. Even more to the point, a message sent via a public relations exercise differs from an advertising message, and will differ greatly from the message a salesperson delivers.

The communication mix continues to be widely taught, and widely referred to by practitioners, even if it has moved on somewhat from its early beginnings.

See also: Schramm model of communication, advertising, sales promotion, corporate reputation, personal selling

The Schramm Model of Communication

The Schramm model of communication seeks to explain how meaning is transferred between individuals, corporations, and others.

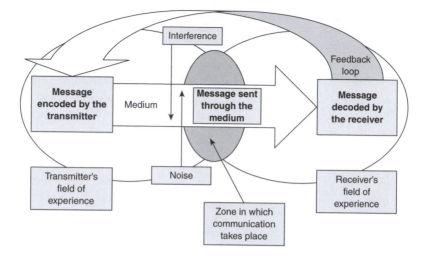

Figure 4.4   *The Schramm model of the communication process*

The most commonly taught and widely used theory of communication is that proposed by Wilbur Schramm in the late 1940s. The Schramm model views communication as a process that takes place between a sender (transmitter) and a receiver: there will be also a message, and a medium through which the message can be transmitted (Schramm, 1948). The receiver may have a method of sending feedback on the message, to confirm that the message has been correctly received and understood, but noise and interference will affect both the ability of the message to get through, and the content of the message. Noise is non-intelligent interruptions in the message process: it can happen at any point in the process, and acts to blot out part or all of the message. Interference is intelligent interruptions in the message process, in other words alternative messages that confuse the receiver.

In 1971 Schramm published an updated version of the model in which the fields of experience of the sender and the receiver were included. The sender's field of experience and the receiver's field of experience must overlap, at least to the extent of having a common language, but in fact the overlap is likely to be much more complex and subtle in most marketing communications. This is the main reason why foreign advertisements are either incomprehensible, or at least seem unintentionally humorous, even when the actual language is clearly understood.

Encoding the message involves translating the original idea into symbols that are suitable for transmission. In some cases the symbols will be verbal (words either spoken or written) and in other cases the symbols will be visual (pictures, logos etc.) while in still other cases sounds that are not themselves words might be used to convey meaning (music, Morse code, animal sounds). Because human beings are not telepathic, such sounds need to be converted back into meaning by the receiver, with consequent risk of misunderstanding or misinterpretation. Using a feedback loop, by which the receiver repeats the message back to the transmitter, is a way of ensuring that the message has been correctly understood.

The Schramm model has considerable appeal. It offers a clear view of the communication process, and accounts for many of the problems inherent in communication. Unfortunately it also suffers from some serious weaknesses, and does not accord well with the modern view of communication.

Communication is currently regarded as a social process, in which there is a co-creation of meaning between those who are communicating. The Schramm model appears to imply that communication is a 'magic bullet' by which information is transferred, albeit with greater or lesser accuracy, from one individual to another. In fact, people are not passive in the process: they consider the communication in the light of their existing knowledge, prejudices, preconceptions and (importantly) they consider the source of the information. All of these factors add to the tendency for the recipients of messages to receive something that often bears little resemblance to what was originally transmitted.

Recently an alternative view of the communication process has emerged. Communications theorists such as Deetz (1992) and Mantovani (1996) see communication as a co-operative process in which meaning is developed between individuals. Their joint perception of the world is developed through a co-construction of meaning, in which dialogue acts as the mediating device. In this model, communication is not something that is *done to* recipients – it is something that is *shared with* recipients.

An analogy for this is shown in Figure 4.5. Reality is represented as a pool of shared meaning into which people have an input. Each person adds something to the pool, and each person takes something out of the pool: what is put in is not necessarily the same as what is taken out, because each individual only takes what he or she wants from the pool. Also, what is put in is mixed with everything else in the same pool, so that the input is transformed.

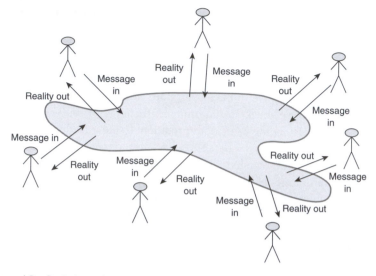

Figure 4.5 *Pool of meaning*

In fact, it does not matter whether the participants in the process communicate or not – they will still re-interpret the message in the light of their existing view of reality. In effect, each participant in the communication process is aiming to shift the shared view of reality in such a way as to favour their own position – relatively few communications are without agenda.

If this alternative view of communication is accepted, it has far-reaching implications for marketers. Any communication that is interactive (personal selling, the Internet, direct mailings) will need to be reconsidered in the light of the model.

See also: *advertising: the weak and strong theories, the communications mix*

REFERENCES

Deetz, S.A. (1992) *Democracy in an Age of Corporate Colonization: Developments in Communication and the Politics of Everyday Life*. Albany, NY: State University of New York Press.

Mantovani, G. (1996) *New Communications Environments: From Everyday to Virtual*. London: Taylor & Francis.

Schramm, W.A. (1948) *Mass Communication*. Urbana, IL: University of Illinois Press.

Schramm, W.A. (1971) 'The nature of communication between humans', in Schramm, W.A. and Roberts, D.F. (eds), *The Process and Effects of Mass Communication*. Urbana, IL: Illinois University Press.

promotion

Advertising: the Weak and Strong Theories

The weak and strong theories of advertising seek to explain how advertising works on consumers.

Advertising is defined as a paid insertion of a message in a medium, and it is probably the most prominent of all marketing activities. Non-marketers often think that advertising is all that marketers do, which is of course not the case: the definition specifically excludes anything that is not paid for, or anything that does not pass through a medium, or anything that does not convey a message. Thus a T-shirt with a message on it is not advertising, since the wearer of the T-shirt is not being paid. Designing an interesting product is certainly marketing, but it is not advertising since there is no direct message.

Advertising forms part of the promotional mix, and current thinking is that it works best as part of an integrated campaign of some sort in which various elements of the mix are brought together. There are things that advertising can do and things that advertising cannot do. In general, it can achieve communications objectives such as informing people about brands, it can create awareness and it can move people closer to choosing one brand rather than another. What it will not do is substitute for a good product, it will not persuade people to buy things they do not need and it will not substitute for good marketing generally.

There has been considerable debate among academics about how advertising works, or even whether it works. The difficulty lies in teasing out the effects of advertising from a number of other possible influences. At the most obvious level, sales may be affected by seasonality, changes in the economic situation in the country, changes in the weather and indeed any number of other factors that have nothing whatever to do with advertising. On another level, the fact that an advertising campaign is about to take place is likely to affect salespeople and distributors: the salespeople will tend to use the upcoming campaign as a useful deal-closer, and distributors are likely to assume that demand will pick up, and will therefore tend to stock up and give the product more shelf space. If retailers do this, sales would be likely to rise anyway, even if there were no campaign – but how are we to know?

Two general theories have emerged from the debate. The first is the **strong theory**, in which advertising is seen as a powerful force in changing people's attitudes. The strong theory assumes that people use advertising as a surrogate for direct experience of the product, using the information as a 'first hypothesis' until they have had the opportunity to try the product out. If this is the case, a heavily advertised product stands more chance of success since it is more likely to be tried out, and also the information gained during the trial will be interpreted in the light of the existing knowledge gained from advertising. In other words, the advertiser has the advantage of the law of primacy: later information is interpreted in the light of earlier information.

The main criticisms of the strong theory are:

- There is little evidence to show that people form strong brand attachments before actually trying the product.
- The model only considers people who have never bought the product before. In most markets, advertising is aimed at people who have already bought the product. This is either to inform them about changes to the product, or to remind them about its quality and thus keep them loyal.

The alternative view is the **weak theory**, put forward by Ehrenberg (1992). The weak theory states that people are only 'nudged' by advertising into buying a particular brand at a point when the individual was already most of the way towards buying it anyway. The weak theory implies that only people who were already planning to buy one of a selection of brands are influenced by the advertising, and then only into choosing one brand rather than another, very similar, brand. The weak theory implies that advertising only reinforces an existing view, rather than having a persuasive role.

The strong theory tends to be more prevalent in the United States, and it is of course possible (even likely) that American experience differs from European experience, given the cultural and geographical distances between the United States and Europe. Research shows that, at least in fast-moving consumer goods markets, people are not usually loyal to one brand but rather have a small group of brands that they will buy on a regular basis: it is difficult for a new brand to break into this group. This would tend to support the weak theory to the extent that the advertising encourages people to choose one brand from the consideration set rather than another: clearly a great deal of effort has to be made to insert another brand in the set, which seems to imply that advertising is not sufficiently strong a force to do this.

Level of involvement undoubtedly has a role to play in people's responses to advertising, since involvement can be interpreted as being a predisposition to seek out information about a brand or a product. Involvement may have a bearing on whether the strong theory predominates or the weak theory (Jones, 1991). In the case of a high-involvement purchase, one would expect that people would seek out information (Blythe, 2006) and are likely to be more affected by the messages since they are seeking out confirmation (or disconfirmation) of their existing information.

As advertising has become more widespread, people have developed increasing resistance to it. Advertising clutter, as it is known, makes it hard for an advertisement to break through and provide the target customers with its message. People are adept at recognising, and avoiding, advertising messages: however, there are circumstances in which people will accept the messages. If the advertisement is about something that the individual finds interesting or is involved with, he or she will accept the message. Equally, people do sometimes enjoy the advertisements as entertainment. Research conducted by Ritson (2003) shows that people have six basic behaviours when the commercial break arrives on TV:

1   **Social interaction**. People discuss their working day, household problems, or general gossip during the commercial break. In this case, the advertisement has only a subconscious effect.
2   **Reading**. Many people keep a book, newspaper or magazine handy while watching TV. During advertising breaks, they catch up with the news or read another chapter. Advertisements probably still have a subconscious effect on the viewer.
3   **Tasking**. Many people carry out household tasks during the commercial break: filling the dishwasher, making a coffee or tea, make telephone calls, or pay bills. The advertisements have low or zero effect, depending on whether the task is being carried out in the same room as the TV set.
4   **Flicking**. Mainly a male activity, this involves switching channels rapidly to see what else is on, or occasionally going to a 'visit channel' such as a news channel for a fixed length of time before returning to the main channel. Only the first and last advertisements in the break have any effect.

5   **Watching an advertisement**. In many cases the advertisements are actually watched, and often family members will comment on the advertisement. The advertisements might be expected to have an effect in this case.

6   **Advertising interaction**. This goes a stage further than simply watching the advert: here the viewers sing along with the jingle, comment on the advert, or even play games such as seeing who can guess the brand name first. The advertisement might be expected to have a strong effect, at least in terms of memorability.

From a marketer's viewpoint, clearly the last two are the most desirable outcomes. Advertisements that are 'zapped' (i.e. the viewer switches channels or cuts the sound) appear to be more likely to have a positive effect on brand purchase than advertisements that are not zapped (Zufryden et al., 1993). This is thought to be because the viewer has to watch at least part of the advertisement to process the content and recognise it as such before zapping it.

Fast-paced advertisements appear to have a positive effect on involuntary attention (in other words they are more eye-catching) but have little effect on voluntary attention (they are no more likely to be watched actively) (Bolls et al., 2003). This again offers support for the weak theory of advertising: in most cases, these unsought communications are not actively processed as communication.

Advertising continues to be an important force, whether weak or strong: the anecdotal evidence for its efficacy is too great to be ignored. Although we only have theories as to how, or whether, advertising works, we do know that firms that never advertise tend on average to do worse than those that do. The exceptions (such as Body Shop) are rare, and in most cases have something else very powerful in the promotional locker.

See also: Schramm model of communication

REFERENCES

Blythe, J. (2006) *Essentials of Marketing Communications* (3rd edn). Harlow: FT Prentice Hall.

Bolls, P.D., Muehling, D.D. and Yoon, K. (2003) 'The effects of television commercial pacing on viewers' attention and memory', *Journal of Marketing Communications*, March 9 (1): 17–28.

Ehrenberg, A.S.C. (1992) 'Comments on how advertising works', *Marketing and Research Today*, August: 167–9.

promotion

Jones, J.P. (1991) 'Over-promise and under-delivery', *Marketing and Research Today*, Nov: 195–203.

Riston, M. (2003) *Assesing the values of Advertising*. London: London Business School.

Zufryden, F.S., Pedrick, J.H. and Sankaralingam, A. (1993) 'Zapping and its impact on brand purchase behavior', *Journal of Advertising Research* 33 (Jan–Feb): 58–66.

Sales Promotion

Sales promotion is the term used to describe short-term incentives offered to customers with the intention of increasing sales in the immediate future.

Sales promotion is usually included in the promotional mix because promotions are intended to communicate a discount and thus create a short-term increase in sales. There are many forms of sales promotion, from cash discounts through to extra quantities of product, free trial packs and free gifts included with every purchase. Sales promotions are typically used as part of a push strategy, i.e. a strategy in which the goods are heavily promoted to members of the distribution chain rather then to the end-customer with the aim of encouraging the distributor to promote the product heavily and push the goods through the distribution chain.

Because producers find that push strategies can be more accurately targeted and are less prone to clutter, expenditure on sales promotion has increased in recent years. Sales promotion that is not of the 'discount' type deflects interest away from price as a competitive tool, thus reducing pressure on profits. Creating the campaign should be based on the 'who do I want to do what?' question (Cummins, 1998). The purpose of the campaign needs to be stated precisely: aiming 'to increase sales' is too vague, whereas aiming 'to move the brand into the consideration set of young people' is something that can be used as the basis for creative thinking.

Sales promotions are used to encourage trial, to trade up (buy the more expensive version of the product), or to use more of the product

sales promotion

185

(perhaps for new purposes): when aimed at distributors, they encourage loading up (increasing stock levels). Sales promotions often only move sales from the future to the present: when the promotion is over, individuals and distributors alike may have sufficient stocks to last for a while, and therefore stop buying. This may not matter if the purpose of the promotion is to even out demand or lock out competitors from shelf space, but it is important to remember that sales promotions are short-term tools for creating short-term effects.

In some cases, customers are required to carry out a mechanic, which is an action such as scratching a card, filling in a form or answering a quiz question. The following considerations apply to designing a mechanic:

- The mechanic should be simple to carry out, or might be seen as too much trouble. A task that is too complex will result in people giving up: on the other hand, those who do carry out a complex task are likely to be the most highly motivated potential customers.
- The feelings of the person carrying out the mechanic need to be considered, paying attention to cultural issues: embarrassing or personally intrusive mechanics should be avoided.
- The mechanic should be comprehensible to the target group, although there is no reason why it should not be comprehensible to an undesirable group. For example, a sales promotion for holidays in France might be written in French, thus excluding non-French speakers.
- The mechanic might be immediate, such as a money-off deal, or delayed, such as a discount off next purchase. Immediate rewards are more appealing, but do not necessarily create future sales.
- The mechanic must be legal. In the UK a mechanic involving a game of chance cannot be dependent on buying something, so someone can demand a scratch card without actually making a purchase. Not many people would do this, of course.

Sales promotion is less common in business-to-business markets than it is in consumer markets. This may be because business buyers are less likely to be swayed by temporary promotions, or it may be that sales promotions do not fit with the idea of building long-term relationships. There may be a role for sales promotion in the form of 'deal sweeteners', small extra concessions offered by salespeople to cement orders and build relationships.

Sales promotions aimed at consumers are diverse, but some of the commoner ones are as follows:

- **Free tastings**. New food products can be promoted in supermarkets by offering small amounts to taste. This is an expensive promotional tool, because the demonstrators have to be paid to give away free product, but it works well in encouraging trial. The consumer often feels under an obligation to buy the product, having accepted the 'gift' of a taste.
- **Money-off vouchers in press advertisements**. The main advantage of this type of promotion is that the managers can see which newspaper or magazine generates the highest number of coupon redemptions, i.e. the marketers can check the effectiveness of one print medium over another. It tends to lead to short-term brand switching: when the offer ends, most people revert to their usual brand.
- **Two-for-one**. Customers pay for the product, but are given an extra one free. This is the same as a generous price discount, so appeals to price-sensitive consumers. Two-for-one offers are useful for disposing of excess stock and shutting out competitors, but they are expensive.
- **Piggy-backing or bundling**. This promotion works by providing a free sample of a product, attached to a complementary product, for example attaching a free cigarette lighter to a pack of cigarettes.
- **Instant lottery or scratch cards**. This type of promotion is commonly used in petrol stations, with the intention of encouraging motorists to stop at the same petrol station.
- **Free gift with each purchase**. Free gifts have ranged from a free Frisbee with suntan lotion to a free sunroof with a new car. This can encourage brand switching, especially when selling to children: children are not price-sensitive, and will tend to keep to their favourite brand unless offered an inducement to switch.
- **Loyalty cards**. These cards reward customers for shopping at the same retailer, or using the same airline or ferry company for travel. Usually the rewards are given as discounts or vouchers against future purchases, but sometimes in-store discounts are available for loyalty card holders, and sometimes points can be redeemed against goods that are only available to card holders. Likewise, some airlines allow frequent flyers to use the Business Class lounges, or to bring a partner on a business flight.

sales promotion

Off-the-shelf promotions are provided by suppliers that specialise in sales promotions. For example, a common promotion is to offer free hotel accommodation to customers provided the customer pays for breakfast and dinner. The hotel is guaranteed some revenue, which makes the promotion relatively cheap for the promoter. Often the vouchers are only valid for off-peak periods, when the hotel rooms might be empty anyway: the hotelier would obviously rather have some income than none, and also the guests may like the hotel and return at a later date, paying the full price.

Off-the-shelf promotions require trust on all sides, since the company offering the promotion has very little control over the quality of the service provided, or the terms on which other people are benefiting from the same offer. If run well, though, off-the-shelf promotions provide benefits to all parties – the promoter gains because customers want the discounts, the firm providing the benefits gains because of the extra business during an off-peak period, and the customer gains by obtaining a cheaper deal.

Joint promotions reduce the costs and increase the effectiveness of promotions by sharing with another firm. The cost of the promotion is reduced, the scope of the promotion is increased because the other firm will contact its own customer base, and the customer's perception of value is often increased. Joint promotions can be linked to a charity or cause, but more commonly they are linked to commercial companies with which the firm has a marketing synergy.

Marketers should be careful not to over-use sales promotions, whichever type of promotion they prefer. Sales promotions work because they offer something unusual: if the product is always subject to a sales promotion consumers will come to expect it. When the promotion ends they will buy other brands, forcing the company to re-introduce the promotion so that the company has simply cut its profit margins for no real gain.

Sales promotions may be ineffective because the temporary increase in sales is followed by a fall in sales, as customers have stocked up on the product. If the purpose of the promotion is to even out seasonal sales, this may not matter, but the following assumptions might be worth considering:

- Loyal customers will stock up on the product and will therefore not buy any more of the product for some time.
- Some consumers who switch brands will switch to another supplier as soon as the promotion ends (Krishna et al., 1991).
- There is a hard core of loyal consumers who will not switch brands, no matter what incentives are offered. These are likely to be the most valuable customers for the brand.

Some people who stock up on the brand will give samples away to their friends (Wansink and Deshpande, 1994). Some people will stay with the new brand – even habitual brand switchers will often stay with the brand until there is some reason to switch (competitors running a promotion, for example). Even the most loyal customers eventually switch brands, if only because their own brand ceases production.

Sales promotions are often integrated with other communications to create a ratchet effect. This is the process whereby sales are sharply increased as a result of a sales promotion, and sustained at the new level by the use of other promotional tools. A clever or controversial sales promotion can create publicity: a sales promotion with a good mechanic can create a database, and a good retailer promotion can support the salesforce in winning orders from retailers.

Of course, integrating marketing communications requires a substantial effort in planning, co-ordination and creative thought.

See also: communications mix, channel management

REFERENCES

Cummins, J. (1998) *Sales Promotion: How to Create and Implement Campaigns that Really Work*. London: Kogan Page.

Krishna, A., Currim, I.S. and Shoemaker, R.W. (1991) 'Consumer perceptions of promotional activity', *Journal of Marketing*, 552 (April): 4–16.

Wansink, B. and Deshpande, R. (1994) 'Out of sight, out of mind: pantry stockpiling and brand-use frequency', *Marketing Letters* 5 (1): 91–100.

Corporate Reputation

> **Corporate reputation is the overall expectation of an organisation's expected behaviours, as held by the organisation's stakeholders.**

Corporate reputation is the overall impression the company gives to its publics. It is usually considered to be part of public relations, and although there is a degree of controversy about whether public relations is really part of marketing or not, corporate image is developed using the trappings and techniques of marketing and therefore it almost always becomes part of the marketing team's remit.

A favourable reputation will have the effect of increasing corporate performance (Deephouse, 1997). This is probably because the reputation makes staff feel proud to be working for the organisation, and also reassures suppliers and customers, which will undoubtedly make the sales staff's work easier. A favourable reputation cannot be copied by other organisations (they have to earn their own reputations), so it becomes a differentiator for the firm (Roberts and Dowling, 1997).

A reputation cannot be categorised as either good or bad. The corporate reputation might be good in some respects and bad in others, or it may be that the organisation has a reputation for something which some people regard positively and others regard negatively. The problem is not therefore one of creating a good reputation rather than a bad one: it is a problem of creating the right reputation so that the organisation's publics are clear about what to expect. Trying to create a 'good' reputation rather than an accurate reputation (good or bad) will result in frustrated expectations.

Managing reputation is more than just an exercise in spin-doctoring. Spin-doctoring is a process of putting a good face on unacceptable facts, whereas managing reputation is a process of ensuring that the facts themselves are acceptable. Good reputation management ensures that stakeholders' experience of the organisation matches the reputation the organisation has, or is looking to acquire. Stakeholders themselves have a role to play in this: staff members (especially those with direct contact with other customers) are crucial, of course, but shareholders, suppliers and customers all talk about the company to other people. Each stakeholder has the power to affect the organisation's reputation simply by saying or doing the right things, or the wrong things, when dealing with other people.

Corporate communications officers have responsibility for boundary scanning. This means being aware of what is happening at the boundaries between the organisation and its stakeholders, with a view to improving the interactions between the organisation and stakeholders. This is similar to the role of marketers, but whereas marketers are responsible for what is done at the boundaries, communications officers are responsible for what is said.

The factors that influence stakeholders, and therefore create reputation are:

1   Direct experience of dealing with the organisation.
2   Hearsay evidence (word of mouth) from friends, colleagues and acquaintances.
3   Third-party public sources such as newspaper articles, TV documentaries and published research.
4   Organisation-generated information such as brochures, annual reports and advertising.

Corporate communications officers have influence over these factors, but the stronger their influence, the less the effect on stakeholder attitude: stakeholders are far more likely to believe the word of a friend than they are to believe a corporation-generated message. The corporate communications officer will try to influence communications about the company, whatever the source of those communications might be: this moves the role away from one of simply managing outgoing communications from the company, and towards one of seeking to create an atmosphere in which even word-of-mouth between people unconnected with the firm still conveys the desired image.

Because reputation affects decision-making on the part of all stakeholders, the reputation of an organisation is both created and consumed by its members. Customers and employees take up their roles in part because of corporate reputation, but they then become part of the communication process each time they talk to other people about the company and its products. There is an element of positive feedback involved – a particular reputation will attract people who feel positive about the organisation and will repel those who feel negative about it. Once inside the organisation, people will act in ways that reflect the reputation. For example, a company with a reputation for treating its staff well will attract managers who like to work in that type of managerial paradigm: these are likely to be managers who, in turn, try to treat their staff well.

Of course, different reputations may be attractive to different stakeholders. Stakeholders are people or groups of people who are affected directly or indirectly by a firm's activities and decisions (Post et al., 2002). For example, employees may be attracted by an organisation's reputation for generous pay scales, but this same attribute might repel a shareholder, who would see it as an attack on profits and therefore dividends. Equally, customers might be attracted to a firm with a reputation for keeping its prices, pay rates and profits at rock-bottom, but this would hardly attract either staff or shareholders. Ultimately it is not possible to please everybody, so managers need to identify who are the key players, and should seek to establish a good reputation with those people.

In practice, organisations acquire reputations rather than develop them. While it may be possible to create a more appropriate or desirable reputation with some stakeholders, this is likely to be a negative move for other stakeholders. In practice managers are unlikely to create a reputation from scratch – they are much more likely to adjust the organisation's existing reputation to make it more attractive to some people, or communicate it better to the stakeholders.

Maintaining a strong reputation pays direct dividends for the enterprise. Research shows that investors are prepared to pay higher prices for the shares of companies with good reputations, even when risks and returns are comparable with other firms in the same industry. Cordeiro and Sambharaya (1997) showed earnings forecasts made by financial analysts were heavily influenced by the non-financial component of the corporate reputation. Surveys of MBA students show that they are attracted to companies with good reputations, which means that companies that are larger and more visible are apparently better to work for. Part of this attraction is the reflected glory of working for a high-profile company, and part of it is about a perception that working for a major company is likely to be more secure and better rewarded.

Whether corporate reputation is part of marketing or part of public relations is still being debated. PR professionals usually regard themselves as being outside marketing, although recognising that there is considerable overlap between the roles: marketers regard public relations as being primarily aimed at customers, whereas corporate reputation is equally powerful for staff and shareholders. Much depends on which definition of marketing one adopts, and where one sets the boundaries: the Kotlerite view that marketing is everything would certainly include corporate reputation management, but others might disagree, regarding reputation management as something in which marketers have a major role, but which they do not by themselves control.

See also: communications, mix, elaboration likelihood model

REFERENCES

Cordeiro, J.J. and Sambharaya, R. (1997) 'Do corporate reputations influence security analyst earnings forecasts?', *Corporate Reputation Review*, 1 (2): 94–8.

promotion

Deephouse, D.L. (1997) 'The effect of financial and media reputations on performance', *Corporate Reputation Review*, Summer/Fall: 68–71.

Post, James E., Lawrence, Anne T. and Weber, James (2002) *Business and Society: Corporate Strategy, Public Policy, Ethics*. New York: McGraw–Hill.

Roberts, P.W. and Dowling, G.R. (1997) 'The value of a firm's corporate reputation: how reputation helps attain and sustain superior profitability', *Corporate Reputation Review*, Summer/Fall: 72–6.

Personal Selling

> **Personal selling is the interactive process whereby a buyer and a seller negotiate an exchange process. It is usually, though not necessarily, carried out in a face-to-face encounter between the parties.**

Personal selling as it is practised is not the same as the selling concept. The selling concept is a philosophy that may have prevailed at one time in industry, and it assumes the following:

- That customers will not ordinarily buy enough of the product without a persuasive sales talk.
- That customers can be tricked or persuaded into buying more of a product than they really need if the salesperson uses the right techniques.
- That the customer will not mind being persuaded, and will still be glad to see the salesperson again.
- That customers' objections to the product or the company are artificial obstacles to be overcome rather than genuine problems to be solved.

This contrasts with the marketing concept, which attempts to anticipate customers' needs and solve their problems profitably. The selling concept can still be found in some companies, but it is a corporate philosophy rather than a set of tactics; most professional salespeople would reject the selling concept as being not only incorrect but ineffective.

Marketers usually think of personal selling as part of the promotional mix. Personal selling is different from the other elements in that it always offers a two-way communication with the prospective customer, whereas each of the other parts of the promotion mix is a one-way communication. From a marketer's viewpoint, this is partly what makes personal selling such a powerful instrument: the salesperson is able to tailor the message so as to concentrate on those issues that seem to be of greatest interest to the prospect. Salespeople can also answer problems and explain misunderstandings as they arise.

Salespeople and marketers often disagree about the relationship between selling and marketing, and this is occasionally a source of conflict between them (Dewsnap and Jobber, 1998). Conflict between salespeople and others within the firm has potentially far-reaching effects: some authors have shown that such conflicts have a direct effect on the buyer's commitment (Tellefsen and Eyuboglu, 2002).

The marketer's view of selling has been coloured for the past 35 years by Peter Drucker's statement that 'the aim of marketing is to make selling superfluous' (Drucker, 1973). He went on to say that there will always be some need for personal selling, but that marketers should aim to produce products that are so ideally suited to the customer that the product 'sells itself'. This attitude towards personal selling has been strengthened by Levitt's statement that 'selling focuses on the needs of the seller; marketing on the needs of the buyer' (Levitt, 1960). The result of this negative view of selling is that marketers tend to adopt one of two general attitudes: at worst, salespeople are associated with the selling concept, and at best they are viewed as a necessary evil, filling in the gaps in the promotion mix by tailoring the communication to fit the prospect's prejudices and preconceptions.

On the positive side, selling has been described as 'the interpersonal arm of the promotion mix' (Kotler et al., 2001); as 'an interpersonal communication tool which involves face-to-face activities undertaken by individuals often representing an organisation, in order to inform, persuade or remind an individual or group to take appropriate action, as required by the sponsor's representative' (Fill, 1995); and as 'the process of identifying potential customers, informing them of a company's offer mix, and finding a match between the benefits offered and customers' needs through personal communication' (Adcock et al., 2001).

These marketer-generated descriptions of personal selling emphasise the information role of selling, and the persuasive role. Figure 4.6 shows the marketer's view of where personal selling fits with marketing.

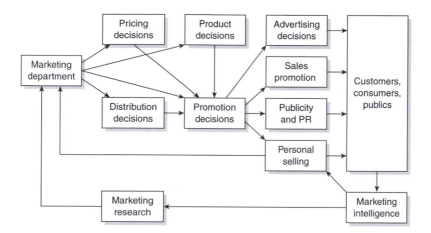

Figure 4.6 *Marketer's view of the role of personal selling*

In this model, marketers make decisions about product, distribution and price, and feed these decisions into the design of a promotional package, eventually developing an integrated communications programme, including personal selling, which is then delivered to the customers. Feedback from customers is collected via marketing research and information provided by the salesforce.

At first sight the marketer's model of the role of personal selling appears to allow for the replacement of selling with other (often IT-based) techniques. Since personal selling is regarded as an expensive option, this viewpoint is wholly understandable. If marketers are right in thinking of selling solely as a communication tool, it is obviously sensible to use other ways of communicating.

Undoubtedly personal selling does have a major communications element, involving as it does a two-way dialogue between salesperson and prospect, but there is a great deal more to personal selling than this. An examination of what salespeople actually do will make this clearer.

Research into sales practice shows a somewhat different picture from that conveyed by most marketing texts. The emphasis in selling practice is not on telling prospects about the products, but on asking questions about the prospect's needs. Persuasive sales talks are not necessary if appropriate questions are asked: questions not only help in finding out about customer needs, but also help to lead the discussion in a particular direction. DeCormier and Jobber (1993) found a total of 13 different types of question in use by salespeople; some of these were for information-gathering purposes, others served to control and direct the discussion. Rackham (1991) categorised questions in four dimensions; situation, problem, implication and need-payoff. In each case the emphasis is on asking the prospect about his or her situation, with a view to finding a solution from among the salesperson's portfolio of products. There are three key elements involved in the selling process: first, finding out customer needs, second finding a solution from among the salesperson's range of products, and third, matching the solution to the stated problem.

Sales trainers and writers have emphasised the problem-solving aspects of selling for many years now: the most successful presentations are those in which the customer does most of the talking (Lund, 1979). Because customers will tell the salesperson exactly how to sell them the product (provided they are allowed to talk), problem-solving is at the core of the activity rather than one-way communication via the salesperson.

In fact, a comparison of the salesperson's activities and the marketer's activities shows considerable common ground: salespeople research customer need, analyse problems, select a solution, negotiate a price, explain features and benefits in way that the customer will find relevant, and arrange delivery of the goods at a time and place that suits the customer. The main difference between selling and marketing is that selling is concerned with individuals and individual relationships, whereas marketing is concerned with market segments.

The salesperson's model of the relationship between marketing and sales will look more like that shown in Figure 4.7. From the viewpoint of the salesforce, it is the salesforce who fulfil customer needs, with the marketing department providing the back-up services of advertising, public relations and sales promotion. Marketers provide information (gained by market research) to the salesforce, and also to the production department, but the salesforce exists to identify and solve customer's problems. They do this using the range of products supplied by the production department.

The salesforce regard themselves as being in the 'front line', dealing directly with the customers. They see themselves as, in fact, the only department that brings in money; everyone else generates costs. Of course, this view ignores the fact they would have nothing to sell if there were no production department, and no invoices would be sent out if there were no finance department.

Many salespeople regard their relationship with their customers as being more important than their relationship with the firm that pays

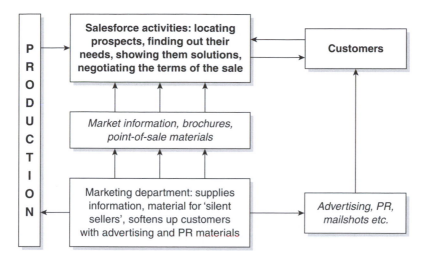

Figure 4.7 *Salesperson's model of the relationship between marketing and selling*

their salaries – research shows that salespeople are often defensive of their good relationships with customers even when this conflicts with instructions from the marketing department (Anderson and Robertson, 1995). Since salespeople spend most of their time with customers, and relatively little time with the company, this is scarcely surprising.

In the salesperson's model the marketing department performs a support function, providing a set of products for the customer to choose from, a price structure for the salesperson and the customer to negotiate around, a distribution system that can be tailored to suit the customer, and promotional back-up in the form of advertising and publicity. Sales promotions might be useful as ways of closing sales (they are sometimes called deal-makers), but the basic problem-solving and decision-making is done by the salespeople when they are with the customer.

It is this problem-solving and decision-making function that distinguishes the salesforce from other 'promotional tools'. The salesforce do not think of themselves as being primarily communicators; they think of themselves as being primarily decision-makers.

From a customer's viewpoint, salespeople also perform a function that goes beyond simply telling them about new products. Although there are undoubtedly salespeople who over-persuade and try to pressurise customers into buying, this approach is usually unproductive. This is for the following reasons:

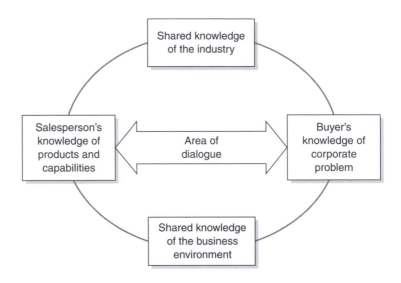

Figure 4.8 *Areas of knowledge and the sales dialogue*

- Most selling situations involve the possibility of repeat business at a future date. This means that the salesperson will be calling again, and would not want to be met with a firmly closed door.
- Most selling takes place in a business-to-business environment, where buyers are generally professionals who are trained to resist a pushy approach. Even in a business-to-consumer situation, most people would show considerable resistance to a bullying or manipulative approach.
- Bullying customers into signing for goods only leads to cancellations once the salesperson is gone.
- This type of high-pressure approach is too emotionally demanding on the salesperson to be sustainable for a long period.

Salespeople will have considerable knowledge of the products in their own company's range, and probably of those of the industry in general. The customer can therefore 'pick the salesperson's brains' for useful information to help in the problem-solving process. The customer's knowledge of his or her unique situation combines with the salesperson's knowledge of products and industry to generate a creative solution. This is shown in Figure 4.8.

For the customer, the salesperson is a source of information, a source of help in problem-solving, and is an advocate back to the supplying company. Good salespeople are also adept at helping their customers through the decision-making process; often this is the hardest part of making a sale.

Overall it would appear that Drucker's view that selling will ultimately become superfluous, and Levitt's view that selling is about the needs of the seller, have encouraged marketers to view selling as 'the enemy'. In fairness, Levitt's statement may have been misconstrued. It would certainly be true to say that the selling *concept* focuses on the needs of the seller. It should also be pointed out that Drucker's statement about the obsolescence of selling could equally be applied to advertising, publicity, or sales promotion: the Drucker ideal appears to concentrate on perfect product development, which is either some way in the future, or buried in the past along with Platonic idealism and the product concept.

See also: communications mix, targeting, elaboration likelihood model

REFERENCES

Adcock, D., Halborg, A. and Ross, C. (2001) *Marketing: Principles and Practice*, 4th edn. Harlow: Pearson.

Anderson, Erin and Robertson, Thomas S. (1995) 'Inducing multi-line salespeople to adopt house brands', *Journal of Marketing*, 59 (2): 16–31.

DeCormier, R. and Jobber, D. (1993) 'The counsellor selling method: concepts, constructs, and effectiveness', *Journal of Personal Selling and Sales Management*, 13 (4): 39–60.

Dewsnap, B. and Jobber, D. (1998) 'The sales and marketing interface: is it working?', *Proceedings of the Academy of Marketing Conference*, Sheffield 1998.

Drucker, P.F. (1973) *Management: Tasks, Responsibilities, Practices.* New York: Harper & Row.

Fill, C. (1995) *Marketing Communications: Frameworks, Theories and Applications.* Harlow: Prentice Hall.

Kotler, P., Armstrong, G., Saunders, J. and Wong, V. (2001) *Principles of Marketing.* Harlow: Financial Times Prentice Hall.

Levitt, T. (1960) 'Marketing myopia', *Harvard Business Review*, July–Aug: 45–56.

Lund, Philip R. (1979) *Compelling Selling.* London: Macmillan.

Rackham, N. (1991) *The Management of Major Sales.* London: Gower.

Tellefsen, T. and Eyuboglu, N. (2002) 'The impact of a salesperson's in-house conflicts and influence attempts on buyer commitment', *Journal of Personal Selling and Sales Management*, 22 (3): 157–72.

Key Account Selling

> **Key account selling (sometimes also called key account management) is the process of managing the relationship between organisations for which the relationship is of strategic importance.**

A key account is one that possesses some or all of the following characteristics:

- It accounts for a **significant proportion of the firm's overall sales**. This means that the supplying firm is in a vulnerable position if the customer goes elsewhere. It also implies that the supplier is likely to be prepared to negotiate significant changes in its methods, products and business practices in order to fit in with the customer's business practices and needs.
- There is **co-operation between distribution channel members** rather than conflict. This places the key account manager in the front line, because he or she will have the main responsibility for ensuring that communication and co-operation happen in the distribution network.
- The **supplier works interdependently with the customer** to lower costs and increase efficiency. This suggests that both parties will need to negotiate at length, and be involved in ongoing discussions throughout a long relationship.
- **Supply involves servicing aspects** such as technical support as well as delivery of physical products. Key account managers will have the responsibility of co-ordinating these support systems.

Because major accounts have the above characteristics, the selling cycle tends to be very long. Selling to major accounts cannot follow the traditional sales approach of finding out needs and closing, which is used in traditional selling situations; it involves a much more drawn-out procedure. Buyers who are considering a major commitment to a supplier, either for a single large purchase or for a long-term stream of supplies, are unlikely to be in a position to make an immediate decision, nor are they likely to be able to make the decision alone. Major account selling will usually involve many decision-makers and several sales calls by (possibly) a team of people from the supplying company. These might include sales people, technical people, even finance experts. Also, major changes in products and practices are often needed, so the key account manager will often have to 'sell' the proposed solution to his or her own company.

This may seem obvious. After all, it seems unlikely that the same procedures used for buying a dozen boxes of copier paper would apply to buying a hydro-electric plant. Small, routine purchases usually only involve one buyer and one salesperson, whereas a major engineering project will involve most of the senior management of the purchasing firm and an equally wide range of people from the civil engineering firm hired to build the plant. It is even probable that a project on that scale would involve government representatives. The sale will obviously not be completed in one call, and in many cases the key account manager will rarely, or never, meet the final decision-maker. The quantity of information that needs to be exchanged will be much greater, so the process will need to go on for much longer. Communication between members of the selling team is also crucial: research shows that the strategic content of communication between team members has a critical role in sales outcomes (Schultz and Evans, 2002).

The monetary size of the order is not always relevant. What is important is that the account has strategic importance for one or both parties. For example, commissioning a designer to produce a new website at a cost of £5000 might be a major decision for a one-man business, whereas a supermarket chain's purchase of £100,000 worth of cornflakes would be a routine deal.

Traditional selling emphasises objection handling, overcoming the sales resistance of the buyer, and closing the sale. This naturally tends to lead to a focus on the single transaction rather than on the whole picture of the relationship between the supplier and the buyer. This may not be important for many purchases, since repeat business might be rare or non-existent. A firm buying a new photocopier may use it for many years before needing another one, so establishing a relationship with the salesperson is hardly important. From the vendor's viewpoint, closing the sale quickly avoids the problem of competitors moving in, which almost always means that the buyer will make the final decision based on price. In key-account sales, on the other hand, the buyer will almost always have to consult with other people in the firm, and it is unlikely that the key account manager will be present for these discussions. Therefore, techniques that work in small-account selling will not work in key-account selling.

When establishing and maintaining a long-term relationship there will be distinct interactions between the parties: these are called **episodes** (Hakansson and Gadde, 1992). The way each episode is handled will depend largely on the past history between the organisations. If the parties know and trust each other, the episode will be handled differently from the way it would be handled if the parties have no history of trust. The possible cases for handling episodes can be broadly categorised as follows:

- Simple episode with no previous relationship. These episodes would involve simple purchases, often in small quantities, or regular purchases of basic raw materials, and are of a fairly standard nature. A key account manager would have no input into this episode.
- Simple episode in a well-developed relationship. Here the relationship facilitates the process, so the key account manager's involvement may be small, or negligible.
- Complex episode with no previous relationship. This type of transaction involves the most negotiation, because complexity in itself generates uncertainty and this is exacerbated by the unknown qualities of the other party to the transaction. Often these purchases are one-offs: for example, a power generating company may only buy one hydro-electric dam in its entire existence, so there is no opportunity to build a long-term relationship with the civil engineers who build the dam. Salesperson involvement is very great, as both an instigator of the process and as a facilitator.
- Complex episodes in well-developed relationships mean that many people from both organisations will need to interrelate (as in the case of the insurance company and the IT supplier mentioned earlier). The previous relationship will inform the progress of events, and the nature of the interaction: the key account manager's role is large, but mainly as a facilitator.

Investing in a long-term relationship usually pays in terms of reducing transaction costs, since there is little or no time wasted on learning about the other party. It also reduces risk by reducing complexity.

All selling, whether key account or small account, has four basic elements that occur broadly in stages. These are as follows:

1 **Preliminaries**. The preparation and ice-breaking stages. These tend to be less important in major sales.
2 **Investigating**. This is where the problem is identified and explored. In major sales this is much more than the simple collection of data.
3 **Demonstrating capability**. This is the stage in which the salesperson shows that he or she has a solution for the problem and has the capacity to put it in place. Because more factors are involved, this stage is much more complex in major sales.
4 **Obtaining commitment**. This is where the buyer commits to the solution being offered by the supplier. In small sales this will usually mean placing an order, but in major sales there will be a number of other commitments which lead towards the final sale.

In small sales, defining the success or otherwise of a sales call is straightforward. If the buyer bought, the sales call was a success – if the buyer did not buy, the call was a failure. In major account selling, there will be several calls: in some cases there might be as many as twenty or thirty calls before a firm decision is made. This means that there is a problem in deciding whether the call was a success: in some cases the buyer might genuinely be moving forward, in other cases a delay might only be an excuse.

Rackham (1987) devised a four-way division of call outcomes to define whether the call had been successful. These are shown in Box 4.3.

Box 4.3   Defining call outcomes

Order   An unmistakeable intention to purchase, for example a signed contract. A buyer saying 'We're going to order from you' is not a sale – only a
signed order form is

Advances   Any event that moves the sale further towards a decision. For
example, a potential customer might arrange for the key account manager
to present the product to a senior manager, or might agree to attend a
demonstration

(Continued)

(Continued)

Continuation The sale process will continue, but no specific action has resulted so far. The customer might agree to a further appointment at a later date. A continuation is not moving the sale on, but equally it does not close the sale down either

No-sale A situation where the customer has shown that no business will result. The customer actively declines the call objective: for example, the aim of the meeting was to meet a senior manager and the customer says that there is no point since the company will not be going ahead, business will not result

The more detailed breakdown of possible outcomes outlined here means that salespeople and their managers can judge more easily whether the sales call has been successful. Of course, a sales call can be successful even if the salesperson's original objectives were not met. For example, if a salesperson visited a client aiming to arrange a presentation to the finance director and was told by the buyer that this would not be necessary because the firm was going to place the order anyway, this would hardly constitute a failed sales call. More subtly, a buyer might tell the salesman that the firm has no need for the product, but that one of their other supplying companies definitely has a need, and an appointment with their buyer can be made immediately. In this case, the sales call has been a qualified success.

In traditional small-account selling, questions are confined to open questions (intended to elicit information and identify problems) and closed questions (intended to move the buyer closer to a decision). In key account selling this is not a sufficiently subtle approach. Because the key account manager is not likely to be present when the final decision is made, he or she needs to 'talk up' the problem so that the initial contact can go to senior management with a convincing plan. Neil Rackham has identified four types of question used in key account selling, as shown in Figure 4.9.

Situation questions are intended to provide background information. Problem questions identify current problems, and implication questions explore the consequences of those problems. Finally, need–payoff questions flag up the benefits of the solution the key account manager is proposing.

promotion

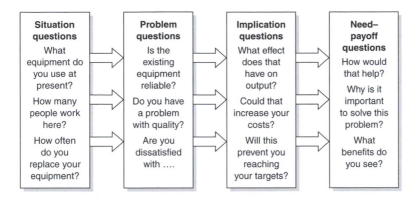

Figure 4.9 *Examples of SPIN questions*

One of the difficulties in major account selling is that the vast majority of calls (even the successful ones) do not result in a sale. Most of the calls move the customer nearer to a sale, but since it may take twenty or more visits before the key account manager has a signed order, it is difficult to judge whether the call was a success. In order to decide whether the call worked, key account managers need to consider the list of possible outcomes shown earlier, and decide which outcome was intended as a result of the call. If the outcome is achieved (or example, an agreement to demonstrate the product to a senior manager), the call was a success. Closing techniques that work in small sales will be counter-productive, since buyers cannot make the decision at this level: a salesperson is better advised to end the sales call with a statement such as, 'I think the next logical step would be for us to talk to your finance director. What do you think?'

Key account selling has created its own rules and problems. Managing key account salespeople is problematic, since it is hard to know whether the sale has really moved on or not, and of course the training most salespeople have is not appropriate for key accounts. Key account selling is not a replacement for traditional selling, of course – it is an entirely independent approach. As time goes on, and traditional salespeople are phased out by the Internet and telephone selling, key account management is likely to be the more prominent end of selling.

Personal selling has always been the Cinderella of marketing, the assumption being that it is about making quick sales at the expense of long-term relationships. This view has actually never been the case, but in recent years the concept of key account selling has gone some way towards dispelling the idea that selling is about high-pressure techniques, fast talking and dubious truthfulness.

See also: corporate reputation, relationship marketing

REFERENCES

Hakansson, H. and Gadde, L-E. (1992) *Professional Purchasing*. London: Rouledge.
Rackham, N. (1987) *Making Major Sales*. London: Gower Publishing.
Schultz, R.J. and Evans, R.R. (2002) 'Strategic Collaborative Communications by key account representatives', *Journal of Personal Selling & Sales Management*, 22 (1) Winter: 23–31.

Integrated Marketing Communication

> **Integrated marketing communication is the concept of ensuring that all messages sent by an organisation carry complementary content in order to ensure that stakeholders develop substantially similar views of the organisation and its products.**

The concept of marketing communication covers a very wide range of functions. Apart from the traditional four functions outlined in the promotional mix (advertising, public relations, sales promotion and personal selling), marketing communications now covers the Internet, ambient media, messages on T-shirts, SMS promotions, word of mouth, word of mouse, e-mail and many more routes.

The problem for marketers is to ensure message consistency across so many differing media. Integration of marketing communications has become a 'hot topic' among marketing academics and practitioners alike, and this is being extended to include all corporate communications

(Nowak and Phelps, 1994). Borremans (1998) identified the following factors as being important drivers for integration:

1 **Changes in the consumer market**:

- The information overload caused by the ever-increasing number of commercial messages
- Advertising in the mass media is increasingly irritating
- Media fragmentation
- Increasing numbers of 'me-too' products, where differences between brands are minor
- Complexity and change in fast-moving consumer goods markets, with increased distances between suppliers and consumers making it harder for suppliers to establish a consistent image
- Increasing media attention on the social and ethical behaviour of companies, putting goodwill at a premium.

2 **Changes in the supplier market**:

- Multiple acquisitions and changes in structure in and around corporations
- Interest of management in short-term results
- Increased recognition of the strategic importance of communication
- Increased interest in good internal communications with employees.

Integration aims to reduce ambiguity and increase the impact of messages emanating from the firm, and also should reduce costs by reducing duplication of effort. Petrison and Wang (1996) suggest that the following factors mean that integration would actually detract from the effectiveness of communications:

- Database marketing allows customers to be targeted with individually tailored communications
- In niche marketing and micromarketing, suppliers can communicate with very small and specific audiences, using different messages for each group
- Specific methods and working practices used for different communication tools will affect the message each transmits
- Corporate diversification means that different branches of the company need to send different messages
- Different international (and even national) cultures mean that a single message comprehensible to all is difficult to achieve without

producing 'lowest common denominator' messages, which have a low impact

- Existing structures within organisations mean that different departments may not be able or willing to 'sing the same song'. For example, salespeople have to deal with customers as individuals: they may not agree with the advertising department's ideas on what customers should be told
- Personal resistance to change, managers' fear of losing responsibilities and budgets. This is particularly true of firms that have adopted the brand manager system of management.

In practice, promotional mix elements often operate independently (Duncan and Caywood, 1996), with specialist agencies for PR, advertising, exhibitions, corporate identity, branding, etc. all working in isolation. Integration may not happen simply because each department has its own budgets and agendas and wants to control its own part of the campaign: in effect, each wants the other departments to come into line with them, rather than change what they are doing to fit with others.

There are nine levels of integration, as shown in Box 4.4. These levels do not necessarily imply a process, or represent stages of development: also, there is likely to be considerable overlap between the different levels.

Box 4.4   Levels of integration

Awareness stage   Those responsible for communications realise that a fragmented approach is not the optimum one

Planning integration   The co-ordination of activities. There are two broad approaches: functional integration, which co-ordinates separate tools to create a single message where appropriate, and instrumental integration, which combines tools in such a way that they reinforce one another (Bruhn, 1995)

Integration of content   Ensuring that there are no contradictions in the basic brand or corporate messages. At a higher level, integrating the themes of communication to make the basic messages the same

Formal integration   Using the same logo, corporate colours, graphic approach and house style for all communications

Integration between planning periods Basic content remains the same from one campaign to the next. Either basic content remains the same, or the same executional approach is used in different projects

Intra-organisational integration Integration of the activities of everyone involved in communication functions (which could mean everybody who works in the organisation)

Inter-organisational integration Integration of all the outside agencies involved in the firm's communications activities

Geographical integration Integration of campaigns in different countries. This is strongest in large multinationals that operate globally, e.g. the Coca-Cola Corporation (Hartley and Pickton, 1997).

Integration of publics All communications targeted to one segment of the market are integrated (horizontal integration) or all communications targeted to different segments are attuned (vertical integration)

These levels can be represented as a ladder, as shown in Figure 4.10 Firms may find themselves at any point on this ladder: there is no reason why a firm should not integrate its publics from the very start, and indeed many small firms do just that.

Part of the reason for separating communication functions is historical. Traditionally, marketing communications were divided into above-the-line communications (meaning advertising) and below-the-line communications (meaning every other form of marketing communication). Originally, advertising agencies were paid commission by the media they placed adverts in (usually the rate is 15% of the billing), and/or fees paid by the client. Advertising attracted commission (above-the-line) and any other activities such as PR or sales promotion was paid for by fees (below-the-line). As time has gone by these distinctions have become more blurred, since many new media do not attract commission and there are in any case a great many ways in which marketing messages are conveyed.

Overall, the advantages of integrating communications almost certainly overcome the drawbacks, since the cost savings and the reduction of ambiguity are clearly important objectives for most marketers. There is, however, the danger of losing the capacity to tailor messages for individuals and

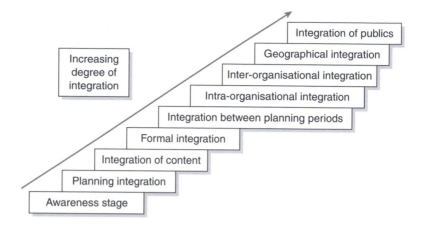

Figure 4.10   *Ladder of integration*

small target groups, and there are certainly some major creative problems attached to integrating communications on a global scale.

See also: communication mix

REFERENCES

Borremans, T. (1998) Integrated (marketing) communications in practice: survey among communication, public relations and advertising agencies in Belgium'. *Proceedings of the 3rd Annual Conference of the Global Institute for Corporate and Marketing Communications*.

Bruhn, M. (1995) *Intergriere Undernehmenskommunikation: Ansatzpunkte fur eine Strategische und Operative Umstetzung Integrierter Kommunikationsarbeit*. Stuttgart: Schaffer-Poeschel.

Duncan, T. and Caywood, C. (1996) 'The concept, process and evolution of integrated marketing communication', in Thorson, E. and Moore, J. (eds), '*Integrated Communication. Synergy of Persuasive Voices*. Mahwah, NJ: Lawrence Erlbaum. pp. 13–34.

Hartley, B. and Pickton, D. (1997) Integrated Marketing Communications: A New Language for a New Era. Proceedings of the 2nd International Conference on Marketing and Corporate Communications. Antwerp, Belgium.

Nowak, G. and Phelps, J. (1994) Conceptualising the integrated marketing communications phenomenon', *Journal of Current Issues and Research in Advertising*, 16 (1): 49–66.

Petrison, L.A. and Wang, P. (1996) 'Integrated marketing communication: an organisational perspective', in Thorson, E. and Moore, J. (eds), *Integrated Communication: Synergy of Persuasive Voices*. Mahwah, NJ: Lawrence Erlbaum. pp. 167–84.

promotion

index

Please note that page numbers relating to Figures and Tables will be in *italic* print

index

index

index

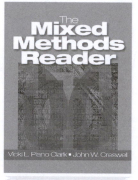

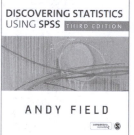

The Qualitative Research Kit

Edited by Uwe Flick

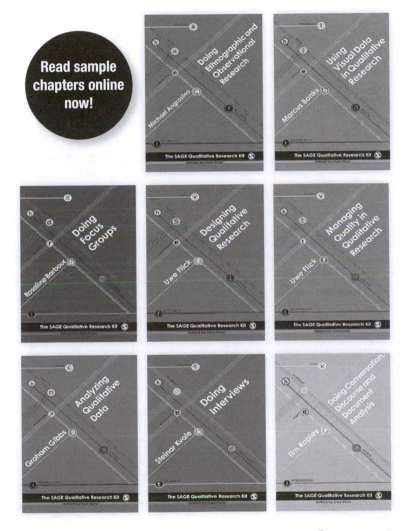

Read sample chapters online now!

Doing Ethnographic and Observational Research — Michael Angrosino — The SAGE Qualitative Research Kit — Edited by Uwe Flick

Using Visual Data in Qualitative Research — Marcus Banks — The SAGE Qualitative Research Kit — Edited by Uwe Flick

Doing Focus Groups — Rosaline Barbour — The SAGE Qualitative Research Kit — Edited by Uwe Flick

Designing Qualitative Research — Uwe Flick — The SAGE Qualitative Research Kit — Edited by Uwe Flick

Managing Quality in Qualitative Research — Uwe Flick — The SAGE Qualitative Research Kit — Edited by Uwe Flick

Analyzing Qualitative Data — Graham Gibbs — The SAGE Qualitative Research Kit — Edited by Uwe Flick

Doing Interviews — Steinar Kvale — The SAGE Qualitative Research Kit — Edited by Uwe Flick

Doing Conversation, Discourse and Document Analysis — Tim Rapley — The SAGE Qualitative Research Kit — Edited by Uwe Flick

www.sagepub.co.uk

Supporting researchers for more than forty years

Research methods have always been at the core of SAGE's publishing. Sara Miller McCune founded SAGE in 1965 and soon after, she published SAGE's first methods book, Public Policy Evaluation. A few years later, she launched the Quantitative Applications in the Social Sciences series – affectionately known as the "little green books".

Always at the forefront of developing and supporting new approaches in methods, SAGE published early groundbreaking texts and journals in the fields of qualitative methods and evaluation.

Today, more than forty years and two million little green books later, SAGE continues to push the boundaries with a growing list of more than 1,200 research methods books, journals, and reference works across the social, behavioral, and health sciences.

From qualitative, quantitative, mixed methods to evaluation, SAGE is the essential resource for academics and practitioners looking for the latest methods by leading scholars.

www.sagepublications.com